NO
MORE
EXCUSES

DISMANTLING RAPE CULTURE

AMBER J. KEYSER

TWENTY-FIRST CENTURY BOOKS / MINNEAPOLIS

For Kaitlin

Twenty-First Century Books
A division of Lerner Publishing Group, Inc.
241 First Avenue North
Minneapolis, MN 55401 USA

For reading levels and more information, look up this title at www.lernerbooks.com.

Main body text set in Adobe Garamond Pro Regular 11/15.
Typeface provided by Adobe Systems.

Library of Congress Cataloging-in-Publication Data

Names: Keyser, Amber, author.
Title: No more excuses : dismantling rape culture / by Amber J. Keyser.
Description: Minneapolis : Twenty-First Century Books, [2019] | Audience: Age:
    13–18. | Audience: Grade 9 to 12. | Includes bibliographical references and index. |
Identifiers: LCCN 2018014574 (print) | LCCN 2018016957 (ebook) |
    ISBN 9781541543959 (eb pdf) | ISBN 9781541540200 (lb : alk. paper)
Subjects: LCSH: Sexual harassment of women—Juvenile literature. | Rape—Juvenile
    literature. | Sex crimes—Juvenile literature.
Classification: LCC HV6250.4.W65 (ebook) | LCC HV6250.4.W65 K4749 2019
    (print) | DDC 362.883—dc23

LC record available at https://lccn.loc.gov/2018014574

Manufactured in the United States of America
1-45224-36607-9/20/2018

TABLE OF CONTENTS

CHAPTER ONE
A TOXIC BREW • 4

CHAPTER TWO
POWER PLAYS • 16

CHAPTER THREE
ALTERNATE REALITIES • 28

CHAPTER FOUR
THE BODIES OF WOMEN • 44

CHAPTER FIVE
I NEED YOU TO BELIEVE ME • 60

CHAPTER SIX
IN THE LEGAL SYSTEM • 80

CHAPTER SEVEN
YES MEANS YES, NO MEANS NO • 98

CHAPTER EIGHT
SPEAKING OUT, STANDING UP • 108

Source Notes   122

Glossary   132

Selected Bibliography 134

Further Information   135

Index   140

CHAPTER ONE
A TOXIC BREW

Late at night on August 11, 2012, a sixteen-year-old girl in Steubenville, Ohio, clutched a red plastic cup full of booze. She wasn't alone. Nearly fifty teenagers had gathered at the home of a volunteer football coach for Steubenville High to drink and party. Most were from Steubenville High School, but some, like the girl, were from a nearby private school. One of the partyers, Trent Mays, a sixteen-year-old quarterback on the Steubenville football team, tweeted, "Huge party!!! Banger!!!!"

Within a few hours, the girl was stumbling drunk and barely able to talk. The party was getting out of hand. The girl became a target of a group of students who taunted her for being drunk. A Steubenville High baseball player urged other boys to urinate on her. The gathered crowd thought that was hilarious. The girl had a crush on Mays, so when he and some other football players from the same school migrated to another party, the girl went with them. She couldn't walk without help. They kept drinking. The girl blacked out. She couldn't remember what happened next.

From pictures, videos, texts, and eyewitness testimony, the police were later able to piece together the story. Someone took off the girl's pants. Her ex-boyfriend, Cody Saltsman, took a picture of her limp, half-naked body suspended in the air between Mays, who held her arms, and another football player, Ma'lik Richmond, also sixteen, who held her feet. Saltsman captioned the picture, "Never seen anything this sloppy lol." He posted it on Instagram, where it racked up comments such as "Whores are hilarious" and "Some people deserve to be peed on."

Mays, Richmond, and another football player put the unconscious girl in the back seat of a car. While they drove to another house, Mays bared the girl's breasts and put his fingers in her vagina. His friend took a video of the assault and posted it online. At the third party, the girl roused enough to vomit and then blacked out again. In the basement of that house, the three boys put her on the floor. Egging

Parties are supposed to be fun social events, but sometimes social pressure to participate in risky or illegal behaviors is intense.

one another on, Mays tried to put his penis in her mouth. Richmond shoved his fingers between her legs. The guy with them shot more video. He took pictures. One showed liquid pooled on the girl's skin. Those pictures made the social media rounds too.

Later, after the actual incident but before the girl went to the police, she wanted Mays to explain the pictures. He texted her, saying, "That was my [semen] on you, not [urine]." He tried to convince her that they had engaged in a consensual sex act (that both participants agreed to have sex). The girl was unconvinced. The morning after the assault, she had woken up on the floor of the basement, naked, surrounded by the three boys. She later said that she was "embarrassed, scared, not sure what to think." She couldn't find her phone or her underwear. She didn't know what had happened. But because of the pictures and videos, which were widely shared on social media, it seemed as if everyone else in Steubenville did.

The day after the assault, the residents of Steubenville were in an uproar. Some blamed the girl for putting herself in a dangerous situation. Others accused her of trying to ruin the reputations of the boys involved. Still others were reeling from the callous and cruel comments made by the many teens who shared the pictures and videos of the assault online. For several days, Mays and other members of the football community tried to delete the incriminating images from the web. They tried to talk the girl out of going to the police. When she finally reported the assault, her family was vilified by many members of the small community.

In November 2012, Mays and Richmond were officially charged with rape. The case rocked the town for months. In March 2013, Mays and Richmond were found guilty of penetrating the girl's body without her consent. They were convicted of rape. Mays served two years in a youth prison. Richmond served one year.

Trent Mays (*left*) and Ma'lik Richmond (*right*) sit in juvenile court during a recess on the second day of their trial in Steubenville, Ohio, in March 2013. The two high school football players were accused, and found guilty, of raping a drunk female partygoer.

SOMETHING'S WRONG IN AMERICA

In the United States, the sexual violation of another person's body is considered a violent crime on a par with homicide. The sentencing guidelines for both rape and murder carry the most severe sentences. Both evoke fear and horror when we read about them in the media or hear a story on the evening news.

Americans abhor rape. At least, they say they do.

Yet throughout the night of August 11, teenagers in Steubenville were watching, taking pictures, and posting videos as Mays and Richmond raped, degraded, and abused their victim. A former Steubenville student named Michael Nodianos watched those videos the same night. He made a YouTube movie of his reactions to what he saw. In his video, he laughs as he gives a play-by-play, saying, "She's so raped right now. . . . He raped her harder than that cop raped Marcellus Wallace in [the 1994 film] *Pulp Fiction. . . .* They raped her quicker than [boxer] Mike Tyson raped that one girl [in 1992]." Nate Hubbard, a volunteer football coach for Steubenville's team, was quick to claim the girl was lying. "The rape [story] was just an excuse, I think. What else are you going to tell your parents when you come home drunk like that and after a night like that? She had to make up something." During the trial, the boys' defense attorneys (lawyers who defend people charged with a crime) claimed that maybe the girl wanted them to do what they did—in spite of the fact that she was clearly unconscious and unable to agree to anything shown in the video footage from that night.

Why were so many people eager to make excuses for the rapists?

David Lisak, an independent clinical psychologist and forensic consultant, says that "there is no domain of crime and violence as fraught with misunderstanding and misconception as that of sexual violence." Americans say that rape is as bad as murder, and yet only 3 percent of rapists will ever serve time. Americans say that rapists are evil people, and yet in case after case, people step forward to blame victims for the crimes committed against them.

What was going on in Steubenville? What is going on with rape in America?

A COMMON CRIME

According to the Centers for Disease Control and Prevention (CDC), *rape* is defined as unwanted penetration of the vagina, mouth, or anus by penis, finger, or other objects. People of any gender can be victims of rape. It is possible for women to rape men or other women. But in the vast majority of cases in the United States, rapists are men and the victims are women. Between 2010 and 2011, the CDC conducted the National Intimate Partner and Sexual Violence Survey. Results demonstrated that rape is shockingly common. In the United States, one in five women and one in seventy-one men will be raped during their lifetime. The frequency of violence against gender-nonconforming people is even higher. According to the Office for Victims of Crime (a division of the US Department of Justice), more than half of gender-nonconforming people will be sexually assaulted during their lifetime. There are more than twenty-eight million rape survivors in the United States alone. But physical and sexual violence is a global problem. The World Health Organization estimates that 35 percent of women have been assaulted by a nonpartner and nearly 70 percent have been victimized by an intimate partner. Few victims ever see their rapists brought to justice.

Why is rape so common in the United States, and why does the legal system fail to punish most sexual predators for their crimes?

The answer lies within American culture. *Culture* refers to the beliefs, ideas, and activities in which people commonly participate together or share as a group. That means entertainment and sports, politics and civic institutions, schools and religious groups. In other words, culture is the shared experience of people in a society. Cultural practices and belief systems around the world have particular ways, both casual and legal, of viewing all forms of sexual aggression and sexual violence, including rape. Sexually aggressive behaviors include things like yelling suggestive comments at women on the street, repeatedly asking someone out after they've said no, or demanding that people send naked pictures of themselves. *Sexual harassment*, a legal term adopted in the United States in 1971, is defined as "uninvited and unwelcome verbal or physical behavior of a sexual nature especially by a person in authority toward a subordinate (such as an employee or student)." This could be a teacher who makes sexual comments about a student's appearance or a boss who tells raunchy jokes at work. Sexual assault is also a legal term that "refers to sexual contact or behavior that occurs without explicit consent of the victim." It could be a person who grabs another student's buttocks in the halls at school or a stranger who shoves his tongue into someone's mouth. Rape is the most extreme and violent form of sexual assault.

> *Sexual harassment* is defined as "uninvited and unwelcome verbal or physical behavior of a sexual nature especially by a person in authority toward a subordinate (such as an employee or student)."

THIRTEEN REASONS WHY

The TV series *Thirteen Reasons Why* is one of the most watched Netflix shows of all time. Its popularity reveals a lot about what American viewers think about sexual aggression and violence in everyday life. In the show, dead girl Hannah Baker has left behind a series of audiotapes that explain to her classmates why she committed suicide.

Her troubles begin when a classmate spreads lies about having had sex with her. As a result, female classmates start calling her a slut. Male classmates begin harassing her, making sexually charged comments, and groping Hannah's body in the halls. One stalks her, taking pictures outside her bedroom window. This sexually aggressive behavior escalates until a male classmate rapes Hannah. Her school counselor tells her to get over it. Her rapist shrugs off his crime and does not face legal consequences. Hannah falls into a deep depression that ultimately ends with her suicide.

Real life has a lot in common with *Thirteen Reasons Why*. In 2014 Dorothy Espelage, a professor of psychology at the University of Florida in Gainesville, conducted a study of thirteen hundred middle-school students. She found that 25 percent of the middle-school girls had experienced sexual harassment. In a similar study of high schoolers, also by Espelage, that percentage rose to 68 percent. Another survey, conducted in 2011 by the Washington, DC–based American Association of University Women, showed that 50 percent of students in the United States, mostly girls but also boys, in middle and high school have been sexually harassed. The harassment was anything but innocent. Perpetrators made sexual jokes, groped and grabbed fellow students, sent unwelcome sexual pictures, and forced victims into unwanted sexual acts.

The negative effects of harassment and assault are profound. Teens who have been harassed often have trouble sleeping, don't want to go to school, change their activities to avoid their harassers, and stop doing well at their studies. Cyndi, a youth organizer with Girls for Gender Equity, says, "[Sexual harassment in school] is a silent word that lingers and spreads through your mind. You are ashamed. You can't focus. You want to speak but you can't. Your voice is trapped in a small, locked box. You are suppressed by your fear, and you can't find help."

GROWING UP IN AMERICAN RAPE CULTURE

In 1963 women's advocate Betty Friedan wrote a groundbreaking book called *The Feminine Mystique*. In it she described the way fear of sexual harassment and assault holds women back. Friedan wrote, "The

Betty Friedan (1921–2006) cofounded and was the first president of the National Organization for Women (NOW). In this photo, she holds up a NOW pin and a Sisterhood Is Powerful button at a NOW national convention in 1970. In the twenty-first century, NOW has hundreds of organizations across the United States.

problem that has no name—which is simply the fact that American women are kept from growing to their full human capacities—is taking a far greater toll on the physical and mental health of our country than any known disease." She and others pointed out that Americans live in a culture that makes excuses for male sexual violence and pretends that assault and rape are normal and inevitable. By the 1970s, feminist theorists had given a name to the constellation of beliefs, ideas, and behaviors that support this view of assault and rape.

They called it rape culture.

Journalist Shannon Ridgway clarifies that when we say *rape culture*, "we're talking about the way that we collectively think about rape." And the reality of being female in America is to constantly be aware of the possibility of sexual assault. In *Transforming a Rape Culture*, coeditors Emilie Buchwald, Pamela R. Fletcher, and Martha Roth point out that "in a rape culture, women perceive a continuum of threatened violence that ranges from sexual remarks to sexual touching to rape itself. A rape culture condones physical and emotional terrorism against women and presents it as the norm."

Terrorism is a very strong word, but in the United States and other cultures, women accept some level of fear as their baseline experience. They know how easily they could be the one in five US women who are victims of rape. And rape culture hurts everyone, including men. Not just because some men are victims of assault but also because the rape-culture expectations of male behavior are narrow, restrictive, and damaging to emotional and mental health. Who wants to be in a situation where they are expected by peers to laugh at rape jokes or to share harassing photos online or to be aggressive toward women? There are a lot of men out there who would rather not be "that guy." Yet the case in Steubenville shows that social pressure to conform to rape culture can be intense.

Most boys and men have women that they care about in their lives. They have mothers, sisters, cousins, aunts, neighbors, friends, and sweethearts. Why would a man want any woman to be afraid to ride the bus home from work or to stay after school to finish a project or to walk home alone from her job? Yet in a rape culture, men are encouraged to be sexually aggressive, and society judges them on their strength and potential for sexual conquest. Women are forced to see them as a natural threat.

This book is for all people who have grown up in the toxic brew of American rape culture. Contorted beliefs about sexual harassment and assault have shaped the way we see ourselves, the way we interact with the people in our lives, and the way we expect others to treat us. They define the world we navigate every day, in school, in families, at work, online, and in just about every other relationship. This book is not an exhaustive history of rape culture, though it does discuss history. Instead, it is a snapshot of twenty-first-century American beliefs about sexual violence.

"Many of us identify as survivors of sexual harassment, assault, and violence ourselves, and we believe we are nearing a tipping point in transforming the culture of violence in the countries where we live and work. It's a moment to transform both the written and unwritten rules that devalue the lives and experiences of women. We believe that people of all genders and ages should live free of violence against us. And we believe that women of color, and women who have faced generations of exclusion—Indigenous, Black, Brown, and Asian women, farmworkers and domestic workers, disabled women, undocumented, and queer and trans women—should be at the center of our solutions. This moment in time calls for us to use the power of our collective voices to find solutions that leave no woman behind."

—Tarana Burke, civil rights activist, and other social justice advocates, Golden Globe Awards, 2018

The language for this discussion relies heavily on the gender binary (the belief that there are only two genders). And it focuses on heterosexual sexual violence (men assaulting women) because rape culture is built on false beliefs about what defines a man and the way he should interact with women. However, the framework for this book acknowledges that gender is fluid and that sexual violence perpetrated against lesbian, gay, bisexual, transgender, queer, questioning, and other (LGBTQ+) peoples is a real and significant problem. To truly dismantle rape culture and create a world free from gender-based violence, definitions of masculinity and femininity must move beyond the gender binary.

This book offers a road map for building a better future in which people of all genders or no gender have sexual autonomy, mutual respect, and physical safety. These solutions include recognizing the historical roots of rape culture in patriarchy (male-dominated society) and misogyny (hatred for women and femininity). It includes believing survivors of abuse, rejecting toxic masculinity, and identifying rape culture in media. It also means reforming laws and criminal justice practices and creating structures for restorative justice. And it includes embracing healthy sexuality and enthusiastic consent, moving toward healthy masculinity, and standing up for one another.

The time for change is now. No more excuses.

CHAPTER TWO
POWER PLAYS

It was no secret in Hollywood that Harvey Weinstein, an influential movie producer, did not like to be told no. He was a powerful man who had the authority to make or break an actor's career. According to some accusers, he could do whatever he wanted. And allegedly, he did. For years no one went public with their claims.

Until October 5, 2017.

That day the *New York Times* published an article by investigative journalists Jodi Kantor and Megan Twohey, exposing allegations of sexual abuse by Weinstein that spanned three decades. A few days later, in the *New Yorker* magazine, Ronan Farrow published the accounts of thirteen women who alleged that Weinstein sexually assaulted them. The stories, told by actors, models, and Weinstein Company employees, had striking similarities. Many reported that Weinstein insisted that they meet him in his hotel room. When they arrived, they alleged that he was nearly naked, demanding massages and sexual acts. He offered to boost their careers in Hollywood if they did what he asked, and his accusers alleged that he threatened to ruin them if they refused. Actors Mira Sorvino and Ashley Judd claim he blacklisted them when they wouldn't give in to his sexual demands. Salma Hayek alleged that he threatened to kill her. Uma Thurman thinks he might actually have tried to arrange an "accident" on the set of the 2003 movie *Kill Bill*. In the following months, more than fifty women accused Weinstein of threatening behavior and sexual assault.

As these accusations against Weinstein came to light, actor Alyssa Milano wanted to know about the experiences of women outside of Hollywood. She tweeted, "If you've been sexually harassed or assaulted write 'me too' as a reply to this tweet." Within hours the internet exploded with social media posts bearing the hashtag #MeToo. Women and girls shared story after story of being catcalled and pursued, being groped and grabbed, being assaulted and violated. The sheer number of stories was overwhelming. Online, some people asked if there were any women who had not been harassed or assaulted in some way. The silence was shocking.

#MeToo

"As a sixth grader, a group of boys held me against a wall as they pulled up my shirt to "see if I stuffed my bra with Charmin or Bounty." The boys barely got a slap on the wrist but I was socially ostracized because I "couldn't take a joke.""
—@CatMilspo, Twitter, October 15, 2017

- -

"And I was blamed for it. I was told not to talk about it. I was told that it wasn't that bad. I was told to get over it."
—@najwazebian, Twitter, October 16, 2017

- -

"When I was a young lawyer, sexual harassment was an all-too common experience. It is a daily reality for many women."
—@KateBrownForOR, Twitter, October 18, 2017

- -

"If you really love me, you'll do it." If, like me, you thought/think that's normal and feeling hesitant and uncomfortable comes with being in a relationship . . . it doesn't. You deserve better. Your feelings are valid. Not being ready is ok."
—@GrapheqDesign, Twitter, October 18, 2017

- -

"I was raped at 15 by a relative. 5 years before he had raped my older cousin, but no one believed her because she was 'fast.'"
—@The_Wilde_Chick, Twitter, October 18, 2017

- -

"Really going to speak up. My rapist/abuser was my boyfriend at the time. Took me years to accept what it actually was."
—@scrappysheppard, Twitter, October 18, 2017

- -

"As an undocumented woman when it happened, I felt like I could not speak up. What if I get in trouble? I thought."
—@julissaarce, Twitter, October 18, 2017

- -

"I was raped when I was 14 and I've told no one about it because I'm a man and she's a woman and no one would've taken me seriously."
—@Geisterwand, Twitter, October 15, 2017

WHO HAS THE UPPER HAND?

Harvey Weinstein was not the only well-known and powerful man that the #MeToo movement called out for alleged sexual assault. Many survivors in the United States and Europe came forward to accuse journalists, politicians, comedians, actors, directors, radio personalities, judges, pastors, TV commentators, celebrity chefs, conductors, corporate leaders, and other prominent men of sexual harassment and assault. It seemed as if the problem was everywhere.

Perpetrators of sexual violence are able to exert their will upon their victims because they are more powerful than their victims. This power is partly physical, but it also comes from the perpetrators' positions of economic power and public influence. When people hold power, they are less likely to be challenged and held accountable for their behavior. In her 1975 book *Against Our Will: Men, Women and Rape*, journalist Susan Brownmiller wrote, "All rape is an exercise in power, but some rapists have an edge that is more than physical. They operate within an institutionalized setting that works to their advantage and in which a victim has little chance to redress [resolve] her grievance. Rape in slavery and in wartime are two such examples. But rapists may also operate within an emotional setting or within a dependent relationship that provides a hierarchical, authoritarian [one dominant person in charge] structure of its own that weakens a victim's resistance, distorts her perspective and confounds her will." As one of Weinstein's accusers put it, "The balance of power is me: 0; Harvey Weinstein: 10."

In most societies of the world, women are the usual targets of predatory men. This is because most cultures are grounded in patriarchy, a form of social organization that puts the majority share of power in the hands of men. Patriarchy views men as superior and women as inferior, with no claim to basic rights. Historically, that meant—and in some societies still means—that wealth, privilege, position, land, and name passed through male family members.

Tarana Burke: "I See You, I Hear You"

In 1996 Tarana Burke was the director of a youth camp for improving the lives of young people. One day a girl at the camp asked to speak with her privately. When they sat down, the girl told Burke that she was being sexually abused by her mother's boyfriend. This revelation triggered Burke's memories of her own sexual assault. It was so upsetting that Burke stopped the conversation and told the girl she should tell her story to someone else. Recalling this moment, Burke said, "I watched her walk away from me as she tried to recapture her secrets and tuck them back into their hiding place. I watched her put her mask back on and go back into the world like she was all alone and I couldn't even bring myself to whisper . . . me too."

Tarana Burke speaks at the #MeToo Survivors March & Rally on November 12, 2017, in Hollywood, California. Burke is the activist who gave the MeToo movement its name.

The interaction continued to haunt Burke. Ten years later in 2007, she launched a movement called Me Too. Her goal was to support women of color like her who are survivors of abuse. She explains it this way: "On the one side, [saying 'Me Too' is] a bold declarative statement that 'I'm not ashamed' and 'I'm not alone.' On the other side, it's a statement from survivor to survivor that says 'I see you, I hear you, I understand you and I'm here for you.'"

Burke went on to become the program director for Girls for Gender Equity, a nonprofit based in Brooklyn, New York, that works to eliminate racial and gender inequities facing girls of color. In 2017 she watched as the momentum of #MeToo exploded. When *Time* magazine announced its Person of the Year in December 2017, the distinction did not go to a single person. It went to a group whom *Time* called *The Silence Breakers: The Voices That Launched a Movement*. Those voices included Tarana Burke, Alyssa Milano, Terry Crews, and the many others who spoke out about sexual abuse under the hashtag #MeToo.

A woman's role was to obey the men in her life, to bear children, and to care for them. Until the twentieth century in the United States and other Western societies, daughters were considered property, owned by their fathers, and transferred to their husbands through marriage. Wives facing domestic violence had no legal protections. They couldn't refuse to have sex with their husbands, and they couldn't file for divorce. They couldn't own and control property or pass it to their children. They couldn't go to school or earn and manage their own money. They couldn't vote or hold positions in government.

FIGHTING FOR SHARED POWER

For centuries, power remained in the hands of men. This didn't begin to change in the United States until the mid-nineteenth century with the birth of the modern feminist movement (also called the women's rights movement) at the Seneca Falls Convention in 1848. At this meeting, more than three hundred people, mostly women, gathered to discuss the role of women in society. They also considered the Declaration of Sentiments, written by Elizabeth Cady Stanton (1815–1902) along with Lucretia Mott (1793–1880), Martha Wright (1806–1875), and Mary Ann McClintock (1795–1884). This document stated that "the history of mankind is a history of repeated injuries and usurpations [taking away rights by force] on the part of man toward woman, having in direct object [goal] the establishment of an absolute tyranny over her." It went on to detail all the rights that were denied to women and concluded, "Because women do feel themselves aggrieved, oppressed and fraudulently deprived of their most sacred rights, we insist that they [women] have immediate admission to all the rights and privileges which belong to them as citizens of these United States."

One hundred people signed their names to the Declaration of Sentiments, including Frederick Douglass (1818–1895), a black writer, activist, and statesman. He saw that the oppression of black Americans and the oppression of women were connected. In spite of

Civil rights attorney and advocate Kimberlé Crenshaw attends the Busboys and Poets' Peace Ball: Voices of Hope and Resistance. It took place at the National Museum of African American History & Culture in Washington, DC, in 2017.

this, the women's rights movement of the 1900s ignored the needs of people of color for most of the century.

In 1989 US civil rights attorney and legal scholar Kimberlé Crenshaw coined the term *intersectionality* to describe how gender discrimination and racial discrimination overlap and interact. She describes intersectionality as "a way of thinking about identity and its relationship to power." Since the 1980s, intersectionality has come to include sexual orientation, gender identity, religion, and social class, in addition to race.

In the simplest definition, feminism is the belief that all genders should have equal access to political, economic, and social power. Extending that idea, intersectional feminism acknowledges that gender equality can't exist unless other imbalances of power are also dismantled. Crenshaw says that it is critical "to sustain a vision of social justice that recognizes the ways racism, sexism, and other inequalities work together to undermine us all."

UNDER THREAT OF ASSAULT

The most privileged and powerful people in most societies are rich, white, able-bodied, heterosexual, and cisgender (when gender identity matches biological sex). Power is at the heart of abuse and assault, so people from marginalized groups (those with less power in society) are more likely to be victims of abuse and sexual assault. The National Crime Victimization Survey and the National Intimate Partner and Sexual Violence Survey, both conducted in 2010, documented these differences. For example, American Indian women are sexually assaulted more than twice as often as white women. People with disabilities are sexually assaulted at more than three times the rate of nondisabled people. Gay men and bisexual people are sexually assaulted more than twice as often as lesbians and heterosexual people. And according to the 2015 US Transgender Survey, nearly 50 percent of transgender people will be sexually assaulted during their lifetime.

> "Simply put, feminism is a movement to end sexism, sexist exploitation, and oppression."
>
> —bell hooks, author and activist, *Feminism Is for Everybody: Passionate Politics*, 2000

Thanks, Wonder Woman!

Merriam-Webster dictionary editors selected *feminism* as the 2017 Word of the Year. It was the most frequent lookup on the dictionary website. Searches for the term spiked in response to several important national events that year. On January 21, 2017, the Women's March on Washington, DC, drew nearly one million protesters. They demanded gender equality and the elimination of gender-based violence and harassment. More than seven million people participated in sister marches around the world.

On April 26, 2016, *The Handmaid's Tale*, a television show based on the 1985 Margaret Atwood novel of the same name, premiered on Hulu. This dystopian drama about women forced into sexual and childbearing slavery raised critical questions about women's rights in modern-day America. On June 2, 2017, the movie *Wonder Woman*, starring Gal Gadot and directed by Patty Jenkins, opened in the United States. One of the highest-grossing movies of the year, it included an iconic scene of Wonder Woman fighting her way across No Man's Land, which became a rallying cry for feminists.

These Guys Are Wild Feminists

During the 2016 US presidential campaign, an audio recording of Republican candidate Donald Trump was released to the media. In it he bragged about sexually assaulting women by grabbing them in the crotch and kissing them against their will. Supporters came to his defense, saying that this kind of "locker room talk" was common among men and didn't mean anything. Debate around the country was heated. Many Americans strongly disagreed that bragging about assault is something to ignore.

Six Americans who disagreed were male student-athletes from a high school in Oregon. They took a stance by posting a photo of themselves in T-shirts from the company Wildfang that said *Wild Feminist*. One of the young men, Rhys Atkinson, said, "It's very important to speak out about [Trump's bragging], because it has to be known that there are men out there that support women and women's rights. . . . Everyone deserves the same rights, and it's not fair that women can be degraded through speech or actions."

Because of systemic racism, ableism, and homophobia (fear or hatred of gay people), law enforcement agencies and the legal system often take crimes committed against people in these marginalized groups less seriously. Victims from marginalized groups know this and are less likely than straight white women to turn to the criminal justice system after a sexual assault. A black woman might fear that police will target and racially profile men in their communities. An undocumented immigrant might be afraid of deportation. A transgender sex worker might fear being further victimized. A poor person may not be able to afford a skilled attorney to represent her in court. Societal prejudices can mean that justice is not equally accessible to all people. For that reason, many people do not feel safe reporting a sex crime, and they may not trust that they will be dealt with fairly.

#METOO IS NOT JUST FOR WOMEN

Actor and former National Football League player Terry Crews knows all about how marginalization plays a role in sexual assault. In the midst of the Weinstein scandal, Crews spoke out on Twitter:

> This whole thing with Harvey Weinstein is giving me PTSD [post-traumatic stress disorder]. Why? Because this kind of thing happened to ME. My wife n I were at a Hollywood function last year n a high level Hollywood executive came over 2 me and groped my privates. Jumping back I said What are you doing?! My wife saw everything n we looked at him like he was crazy. He just grinned like a jerk. . . . I decided not 2 take it further becuz I didn't want 2b ostracized — par

> 4 the course when the predator has power n influence. I let it go. And I understand why many women who this happens to let it go. Who's going 2 believe you? (few) What r the repercussions? (many) Do u want 2 work again? (Yes) R you prepared 2b ostracized? (No).

Terry Crews attends a charitable event in Los Angeles, California. Crews has spoken publicly about his own experiences as the victim of sexual harassment. In the fall of 2018, Crews settled a lawsuit with the Hollywood agent who had abused him.

Terry Crews is a large, physically tough person. Some wondered why he didn't just punch the man. In an interview on *Good Morning America*, shortly after posting his tweet, Crews explained that as a black man in America, if he responded with physical force he would have been seen as a thug. Crews knew that if he had been white, he could perhaps have responded differently. But the man who assaulted him was a powerful, white film executive, so the risks were too high. Crews faced two key power differentials: The first was race. The second was that his abuser had so much power in the movie business that he could damage Crews's career.

"People need to be held accountable," said Crews during the *Good Morning America* interview. "It's an abuse of power. . . . This guy is one of the most powerful men in Hollywood. And he looked at me at the end [after he had groped Crews] as if to say *Who's going to believe you?* I understand why [women] won't come forward. . . . When a person of power breaks that boundary [of personal space and safety], violates that boundary, you are a prisoner of war. . . . I had to tell my story so that other people could be free [to tell their stories too]."

A NEW DAY

Shortly after the allegations against Harvey Weinstein surfaced, celebrities gathered in Beverly Hills, California, at the 2018 Golden Globe Awards to celebrate international and American achievements in film and television. But they did more than talk about movies.

A group of influential women in Hollywood used this platform to launch a movement called Time's Up in collaboration with social justice activists including Tarana Burke, the creator of the #MeToo hashtag. Time's Up declares, "The clock has run out on sexual assault, harassment and inequality in the workplace. It's time to do something about it." In an open letter signed by several hundred Hollywood stars, the women of Time's Up expressed their intentions, saying, "We also want all victims and survivors to be able to access justice and support

Oprah Winfrey accepted the 2018 Cecil B. DeMille Award during the Golden Globe Awards in January 2018 in Beverly Hills, California. She used the moment to speak movingly and forcefully in support of the #MeToo movement.

for the wrongdoing they have endured. We particularly want to lift up the voices, power, and strength of women working in low-wage industries where the lack of financial stability makes them vulnerable to high rates of gender-based violence and exploitation."

One of the women involved in Time's Up is actor and media superstar Oprah Winfrey. She gave a powerful speech during the Golden Globe Awards, saying of the #MeToo movement, "A new day is on the horizon! And when that new day finally dawns, it will be because of a lot of magnificent women . . . and some pretty phenomenal men, [who are] fighting hard to make sure that they become the leaders who take us to the time when nobody ever has to say 'me too' again."

CHAPTER THREE
ALTERNATE REALITIES

Scenario 1. You've stayed late after school. Pretty much everyone else has gone home. The main office is dark, and the door is locked. You're heading down the hallway, but as you go, one of your male teachers suddenly appears and calls out to you. "I'll walk out with you," he says. What do you do?

Scenario 2. It's after ten. You went to get pizza with friends. Now you're walking home alone. Down the block, two men walk toward you. They're loud, joking and messing around, and taking up space. What do you do?

Scenario 3. You're riding the subway home after work. At each stop, people get off and the car empties, until finally, only two people are left—you and a man one row over. He gets up and walks toward you. What do you do?

If you're a straight, white guy reading this, the answers might be pretty straightforward. You chat with the teacher about the upcoming exam. You keep on going down the sidewalk and maybe say hello to those guys. You kick back and wait for your subway stop.

If you're female or a member of another marginalized group, the thought process is a whole lot different. Who is the teacher? Has he given you a bad vibe before? Do other girls say to keep your distance from him? Can you cross the street without the guys noticing you? Should you duck into the Quickie Mart on the corner and wait until they pass? Can you move into the next subway car where there are more people? Is it worth getting off a stop early?

Certain segments of society—usually (but not always) straight, white men—rarely need to make threat assessments. They don't generally worry about their physical safety. They don't get catcalled on the street. Strangers don't sit right next to them when there are twenty empty seats in a subway car.

Many women and people in other marginalized groups rehearse disaster scenarios all the time. They walk to their cars at night looking over their shoulders. They consider how long it takes to unlock and

People react to situations and settings differently, depending on age, race, gender, and other identity demographics. An empty parking lot may be a perfect place for some people to skateboard at night. For others, it can be a terrifying spot, where the threat of sexual assault is very real.

relock the front door of their apartment and take out their keys ahead of time. They avoid alleys and cross the street to avoid confrontations with male strangers. They stay over at a friend's house if it feels too late to ride the bus or take the subway. Women make these observations and calculations and emergency plans so often that it's second nature. They don't talk about it a lot, because why bother? It's something women have to do. But it takes a lot of mental and emotional energy to be on alert all the time. It influences the way women and other marginalized peoples spend their time and where they choose to go and how they plan their daily activities. When harassment and the threat of sexual assault are everywhere, it limits women in ways that straight, white men aren't limited. And most men don't even realize it.

PINK, BLUE—WHAT DO YOU DO?

What does it mean to be a man? What does it mean to be a woman? It seems as if humans have always been debating our differences. Are they real? If so, where do they come from? Does it matter that there are pink aisles and blue aisles in stores that sell kids' toys and clothes? Do innate differences explain the power dynamic in male-female relationships and encounters?

Many people have made the claim that men and women are by nature totally different creatures. This claim is based on the biological differences between the sexes, including different sex chromosomes (usually XX for females and XY for males), different ratios of sex hormones (more estrogen for females and more testosterone for males), and different reproductive body structures (usually a uterus, ovaries, and vagina for females and a penis and testicles for males). But gender—a person's sense of whether they identify most strongly as a female, a male, or in between—doesn't always match with genetic and anatomical sex. Intersex individuals have alternate combinations of internal and external reproductive organs. For example, they might have both a penis and ovaries. Transgender individuals experience a distinct mismatch between their gender identity and their physical body.

Gender identity is closely related to gender norms, which are a set of characteristics and behaviors that a society assigns to individuals. Gender norms (or stereotypes) differ across cultural traditions. But within each society,

Gender norms are reinforced at many levels, including color choices. Historically, pink has signified "girl" and blue has signified "boy." As American consumers begin to demand gender-neutral options, clothing and toy manufacturers are offering gender-neutral products in gender-nonspecific colors.

gender norms define what it means to be a woman (feminine) and what it means to be a man (masculine). Typically, gender norms are binary, allowing for only two options. Broadly speaking, femininity refers to the characteristics and dress codes that people in a particular time and place give to women. These may include a nurturing personality, physical softness, submissive behavior, wearing dresses and high heels, and a preference for focusing on relationships. Masculinity describes a culture's view of men and manhood. This might include an aggressive personality, physical toughness, dominant behavior, wearing short hair, and a preference for focusing on career advancement.

Is there really a biological basis for these gender stereotypes? Neuroscientists have found some differences between the brains of women and men. Specifically, a region of the prefrontal cortex called the straight gyrus is larger in women than in men. This finding prompted some to think that this region of the brain is partly responsible for gender differences. To test this idea, Jessica Wood and Peg Nopoulos, professors at the University of Iowa in Iowa City, looked at the straight gyrus in children. They were surprised to find that the straight gyrus was actually bigger in boys than in girls. What happened between childhood and adulthood to change the size of the straight gyrus?

Neuroscientists know that the brain is flexible and adaptable. It changes over time based on the input it receives. Some of that input is shaped by a culture's gender norms. Lise Eliot, a professor of neuroscience at the Rosalind Franklin University of Medicine and Science in Chicago, Illinois, says, "Individuals' gender traits—their preference for masculine or feminine clothes, careers, hobbies and interpersonal styles—are inevitably shaped more by rearing and experience than is their biological sex. Likewise, their brains, which are ultimately producing all this masculine or feminine behavior, must be molded—at least to some degree—by the sum of their experiences as a boy or girl."

Dr. Colleen Clemens, the director of women's and gender studies at Kutztown University in Pennsylvania, expands on Eliot's research. She says, "Gender identity is a deeply held feeling of being male, female, or another gender. People of different genders often act differently, not because of biological characteristics but because of rigid societal norms created around femininity and masculinity."

ON THE PLAYGROUND

Gender norms that shape how our gender identity develops kick in as soon as we're born. It starts with the way our parents dress us, the toys they buy for us, and the way they talk to us. We experience pressure to conform to gender norms in all aspects of life—in our families, in our communities, in the books we read and the shows we watch, and in our schools.

Donald Trump was elected president of the United States in November 2016. By this time, the audiotape of him bragging about grabbing women by the genitals had made international news. The effect of this demeaning talk about women reverberated through all levels of society—even on the playground. Rachel Simmons is the cofounder of Oakland-based Girls Leadership. This organization teaches girls to become confident, outspoken leaders. Simmons started hearing from parents and counselors. At one elementary school, boys were playing a game they called Trump Tag. The game involved

> "I'm automatically attracted to beautiful [women]. . . . I just start kissing them. It's like a magnet. Just kiss. I don't even wait. And when you're a star, they let you do it. You can do anything. . . . Grab 'em by the [crude word for female genitals]. You can do anything."
>
> —Donald Trump, US presidential candidate, *Access Hollywood*, videotaped conversation, 2016

chasing girls and grabbing them between the legs. At a middle school, boys had declared the second day of the school week to be Grab Tits Tuesday. During a fire drill at a nearby high school, several boys urged one another to grope female students in the buttocks while they lined up outside.

Why does this matter?

Say you're one of the girls at the receiving end of Trump Tag, and say you complain to an adult. The chances are pretty good that someone will tell you that it's "just boys being boys." When adults say "boys will be boys," they imply that grabbing, pinching, or tweaking other people's bodies is a natural thing for boys to do. They are saying that it's nothing to worry about or interfere with. Another thing they might say is that the girl should just "ignore it." When adults believe that boys are hardwired to grope, that often means they won't hold boys responsible for their actions or discipline them. Girls are expected to suck it up and deal with sexual aggression on their own.

> "The argument that 'boys will be boys' actually carries the profoundly anti-male implication that we should expect bad behavior from boys and men. The assumption is that they are somehow not capable of acting appropriately, or treating girls and women with respect."
>
> —Jackson Katz, co-founder of Mentors in Violence Prevention, *The Macho Paradox*, 2006

Another thing girls hear a lot is that when a boy teases or torments her, it means "he likes her." Equating aggression to affection teaches young people that violence and love go together. This makes it more likely that boys will grow into men who will violently insist on getting what they want from women. It conditions girls to accept abuse as normal. It tells them that their consent doesn't matter. Rachel Simmons says, "It is not only acts of harassment that harm girls. It is the expectation that they not resist them."

And what about the boys?

They're learning a lot too.

When a US presidential candidate is caught on tape saying that he can grab, grope, and kiss women whenever he wants, then boys get the message that they can grab girls freely too. They get implicit permission (unspoken approval) from one of the planet's most powerful men to think of girls' bodies as objects they can handle at will. When a president and other adults make excuses for sexually aggressive behavior by calling it "locker room talk" or saying that "boys will be boys," that's a free pass for boys to harass female classmates. And that's how they come up with Trump Tag and Grab Tits Tuesday.

These messages and behaviors also communicate to other boys that there is only one true way to be a boy, and that's to be a groper. However, the work of researchers such as Lise Eliot shows that boys aren't born this way. So why are boys the ones playing Trump Tag? Harris O'Malley is a contributor to the Good Men Project, an organization that encourages men to dismantle stereotypes about male identity and masculinity. He says the expectation of male violence is a part of toxic masculinity. According to O'Malley, the term *toxic masculinity* is a way to talk about "a narrow and repressive description of manhood, designating manhood as defined by violence, sex, status and aggression."

In the face of toxic masculinity, boys and men are forced to make difficult choices. Binary gender norms pit men and women against each other. For example, if men are strong, then women are weak; if men are tough, then women are sensitive. Men can choose to suppress parts of their personality, such as vulnerability and gentleness.

> "How can we hope to stop violent sexual behavior if violence and sexuality are still considered primary virtues of manhood?"
>
> —Ryan Douglass, writer and advocate, *Huffington Post*, 2017

> "We need to create space for boys to know that there is more than one path to becoming a man, and that those paths do not have to lead to violence."
>
> —Colleen Clemens, director of Women's and Gender Studies at Kutztown University in Pennsylvania, Teaching Tolerance, 2018

By doing so, they gain the privilege of being viewed as a "real" man. If they show vulnerability and gentleness or other stereotypically female characteristics, they risk being viewed as weak, girlish, or gay. They face rejection, public shaming, and violence, often from their peers. As journalist Jill Filipovic puts it, "Male sexuality, and maleness in general, are socially enforced by requiring men to be Not Women." Both homophobia and misogyny intersect with this phenomenon.

Dorothy Espelage's study of sexual harassment and bullying among middle schoolers demonstrated a hierarchy of bullying behavior. When boys who exhibited stereotypically female characteristics were taunted with homophobic slurs, they were more likely to sexually harass their female peers. Espelage interpreted this as an attempt by those boys to prove their masculinity. In this way, the negative effects of toxic masculinity trickled down a social hierarchy. Boys who fit the narrow norms of acceptable masculinity bullied boys who were less stereotypically masculine. Those boys, in turn, bullied girls, who bear the brunt of patriarchy's strictly enforced gender roles.

Healthy masculinity, in contrast to toxic masculinity, means that a person is comfortable in their own masculine identity. They don't need to punish the expression of femininity in others. In addition, they can embrace and appreciate elements of femininity within themselves. Alok Vaid-Menon is a gender-nonconforming poet and activist who asks people to consider this question: "What feminine part of yourself did you have to destroy in order to survive in this world?"

A Boy's Perspective

Carlos is sixteen. He lives with his family in a small town in the Midwest. He thinks deeply about what it means to be a man in the United States in the twenty-first century. This is an excerpt from a conversation with him.

Q: What are the pressures society puts on men? Do you feel as if you have to act a certain way?

A: It's more the cultural perception of being "weak." You are seen as a [wimp] if you are depressed. You are seen as a [wimp] if you have anxiety. Especially as a man. Girls, I feel like we see that as normal, for them to have anxiety and depression and weight issues. But if you're a dude and you feel like you're too skinny or too fat, you're a [wimp].

Q: What do you think about masculinity? Does it have limits?

A: I . . . hate masculinity. I hate it. It's such a toxic mindset to have to carry yourself a certain way, to have to act a certain way, to have to look a certain way, just because you have a penis. It kind of ruins your whole life.

Q: What do you think about feminism?

A: I love feminism—it's important. But I hate the super-reactionary, "all men are bad," third-wave feminism that was rampant on the internet when I was thirteen. It ruins the idea of feminism, which addresses serious issues around gender equality. But they're right about toxic masculinity. It changes the way that you act. You're trying to be manly and impress people, and you don't even realize it until you are called out for being a total a$*hole.

WHAT ABOUT THE GIRLS?

Trump Tag and Grab Tits Tuesday are forms of sexual assault. Making sexually explicit comments and catcalling constitute sexual harassment. (It is sometimes called street harassment when perpetrated by strangers in public places.) Both are expressions of toxic masculinity that can make daily life hostile and frightening for women.

My Name Isn't Hot Momma

In 2017 Netflix launched a reboot of *She's Gotta Have It*, director Spike Lee's first movie, from 1986. In the opening episode of the reboot, a stranger on the street harasses main character Nola Darling. When she blows him off, he calls after her again. Again, she tries to deflect him, but he grabs her wrists and swears at her.

Nola pulls free and channels her hurt and rage into art. She plasters her Brooklyn, New York, neighborhood with posters of herself that say things like "My Name Isn't Mamacita." (*Mamacita* is a Spanish-language term that translates literally as "mommy" or "little mama." Yet it isn't used to talk about real mothers in real families. Instead, it has sexual overtones and usually means something like "hot momma." On the street, from a stranger, it is inappropriate and harassing.)

Protest artist Tatyana Fazlalizadeh created Nola's art for the show. Her real-life street protest art, *Stop Telling Women to Smile*, was the inspiration for the show's artwork. Fazlalizadeh echoes the experience of many women when she says, "[The art] was informed by my experiences with street harassment. It's been a big part of my life for a very long time. And, because I'm black, the street harassment and the sexual harassment that I receive is often overlapped with racism. . . . It just kind of clicked to me to create art about this experience that I have all the time and to create it in the space where it happens."

Tatyana Fazlalizadeh attends the 2018 unveiling of her mural portrait of Trayvon Martin in New York City. In 2012, when he was seventeen, Martin was killed by George Zimmerman, a neighborhood watchman. Zimmerman stood trial and was acquitted of second-degree murder (intentional murder that is not premeditated). Americans were deeply divided over the case, disagreeing about its racial dynamics and about Florida's stand-your-ground law (the right to defend oneself with deadly violence). Martin was unarmed when he was killed.

India, a freshman in high school, remembers:

I was standing in the subway, feeling confident, listening to
my music on my way to Union Square [in San Francisco],
holding onto the pole when suddenly, out of nowhere, this
middle-aged guy groped me. He just completely went for
it and squeezed my [buttocks] as if I were just this public
thing there for anyone to grab onto—like that pole I was
grasping. I really freaked out. . . . I wanted to turn around
and scream. . . . It was a crowded train and what would
everyone think? My shorts were too short and my tank
top was too tight. I knew everyone would think I was a
slutty teenage girl and I was asking for it. . . . The moment
before this man grabbed me, I felt good and didn't care
about anyone's criticism or judgement. . . . I didn't want to
be touched and made to feel like a slut who deserved it—I
didn't want to be made to feel like I wasn't even a person.

Krystal, a junior in high school, remembers:

I took the bus uptown to the Bronx [a neighborhood in
New York City] and this older guy sat next to me. I tried to
do homework, and I could feel him staring at me, but we
didn't talk. Everything was good. Then, as I was about to
get off, he asked, "Can I get your number, sexy?" I simply
said, "No." It's my number and I'm seventeen, and I don't
want to give my info out to some thirty-five-year-old on
the uptown bus. "You a THOT anyways," he shouted at
me. . . . To him, because I rejected him, I was one of "That
Ho Over There." I'm a piece of [excrement], a slut, trash
because I didn't want to give a stranger my phone number.
He spit degrading words at me to make himself feel like a

man again. And it made me want to punch a wall because it never ends. Truth is, this is what we hear every day. Girls are shamed and humiliated daily by men like that in public places because they don't smile or strut or look in their direction or give out phone numbers.

SCHOOL SHOULD BE A SAFE PLACE

Sexual harassment doesn't just happen on the streets. It also occurs at school. A law known as Title IX of the Education Amendments of 1972 is meant to protect students. It states, "No person in the United States shall, on the basis of sex, be excluded from participation in, be denied the benefits of, or be subjected to discrimination under any education program or activity receiving Federal financial assistance."

Title IX was passed into law in the early 1970s to prohibit sexual harassment and other threats to a safe learning environment for all students in public schools. The law also ensured that public schools in the United States offer equal access to organized sports for girls.

Title IX is best known as the law that opened organized school sports to girls. The law also impacts other important aspects of life at schools and colleges. It requires schools to provide a fair, welcoming, and safe environment for learning. It prohibits behaviors that create a hostile or unsafe environment. Title IX protects a student if a teacher or school employee asks the student for sex in exchange for a grade or a privilege, or if that teacher or employee threatens to punish the student for not complying with demands for sex.

Title IX also forbids significant hostile behavior such as sexualized comments, unwelcome touching, demeaning graffiti, and degrading jokes made by other students or staff. If your school is failing students in these ways, you have very specific rights. Under Title IX, your school is required to

1. have a sexual harassment policy, which you have a right to see;
2. have a clear procedure for filing complaints;
3. have a staff member designated to ensure compliance with Title IX; and
4. do something.

That's right. Your school is required to actually do something if sexual harassment is creating an environment where you can't learn.

Schools often fail to enforce Title IX because they have an incentive (reason) to underreport harassment claims and to cover up sexual assault. For example, in 2005, the group Girls for Gender Equity launched a voluntary campaign to combat student-to-student sexual harassment in New York City public schools. One principal refused to be included in the campaign. He said, "Absolutely not! My school will not be labeled the 'sexual harassment school.' . . . If [our school] puts this in place, and the other schools in our district don't, then our incident reports [official complaints] will go up and no one else's will. That will ruin this school's reputation." The principal chose to ignore student safety rather than participate. He didn't want to have parents pull their students from the school, which would have led to a loss of state funding for the school. Reactions like this don't help students feel safe enough to speak up about harassment.

Pretending a problem doesn't exist won't lead to solutions. If sexual harassment creates a hostile environment at your school, consider working with a supportive staff member to take a survey of students. Check out the one developed by teens working with Girls for Gender Equity in the book *Hey, Shorty!* The survey is meant to be given to everyone in the school and provides an anonymous way for students to share their experiences. The results can be used to assess how serious the problem of sexual harassment is at your school.

If harassment is creating a hostile environment, you have a right to push for change. Two organizations—End Rape on Campus, and the Center for Changing Our Campus Culture—offer resources for colleges across the United States. If you're in high school, rally students

Unwanted sexual attention is a violation of human rights. Around the world, women are protesting sexual violence and demanding the right to say no. This woman holds a sign at a protest in the United Kingdom.

to ask your counselor to bring in speakers who can talk to your school about safety, equality, and inclusion. If you feel as if no action is being taken, contact the American Civil Liberties Union (ACLU). This national group defends citizens against violations of civil rights, including sexual harassment.

Above all, work on getting comfortable with calling out behaviors that create hostile environments for yourself and others. Girls for Gender Equity suggests using clear, direct words to tell the person to stop. Saying "I don't want you to touch my hair" or "I don't like what you are saying to me" in a firm voice is very effective. It catches the person's attention and leaves no room for negotiation. Many girls are trained from an early age that being nice is important, so a girl or woman's first impulse in facing harassing behavior is often to use soft language. She may say, "That's very flattering, but I'm not interested," instead of "I don't like what you are saying." But this gentle wording can be (and often is) misinterpreted by the harasser being coy or flirtatious. If you're being harassed, fight the urge to make excuses or to smile while saying, "Oh, stop." This undermines the seriousness of what you are communicating and can be interpreted as flirting. The harasser may decide to just be louder and more persistent to get you to give in.

The ability to be blunt and set firm boundaries takes practice. Some bystander intervention programs have participants practice shouting "No! No! No!" over and over at the loudest possible volume. To prepare her daughters for dealing with harassment, author Barbara Kingsolver had them practice these responses: "Don't say that to me. Don't do that to me. I hate it." In a rape culture, harassers believe they have a right to exert their power over others. The words that girls and women use to push back have to be loud and clear.

CHAPTER FOUR
THE BODIES OF WOMEN

In the United States, the bodies of women are on display everywhere. Images of breasts and thighs and bare backs and buttocks are plastered on billboards and in store windows. Glossy magazines are full of sleek, long-limbed female bodies with very little clothing. Online links to pornographic videos describe body parts and what gets done to them. Famous pop stars and actors appear at awards shows in gowns that are little more than slips of fabric. Hollywood websites debate underboob and sideboob and wardrobe malfunctions.

What does it mean when the American Apparel brand creates an ad that shows a woman in a bodysuit, legs spread wide, with the caption "Now Open"? What about a high-fashion photo in *Details* magazine in which a woman's naked body is used as a table to display shoes, belts, and sunglasses? Companies use the bodies of women to sell everything from perfume to alcohol to fame and fortune. They imply through imagery, "If you like this breast, you'll like driving this car" and "Breasts are great and so is beer." Advertising has a long history of associating sexy images with objects for sale. In doing so, the ads transform women's bodies into objects that exist to be used and consumed, usually in a way that satisfies someone else—a man.

This is especially true for black women in America. During the height of the slave trade, white landowners in the colonial United States forcibly transported Africans to their plantations. Considered property, these enslaved people were, quite literally, objects for consumption. They were bought and sold, worked to death in the fields, and killed for breaking rules, great or small. Slaveholders often raped black women and sold their children to far-distant plantations. Because of this history, black women of the twenty-first century are often objectified more than white women.

The message of woman-as-object is reinforced in many other parts of popular culture—the shows we watch, the music we dance to, the books we read, and the art we experience. Eighteen-year-old Odley was a young girl in 1999 when she first saw the music video for the song "Big Pimpin'" by the rapper Jay-Z. She describes her first impression:

All the beautiful women, their amazing swimsuits, smiling, dancing around the men while champagne was poured on their faces. It seemed great to me at the time. I was a young girl just dancing to the beat, drooling over the glamorous lifestyle, and laughing—completely unaware of what I was really hearing and seeing. As I got older, I started to actually listen to the lyrics and I began to understand what was being said. . . . I realized that this whole entire thing is about spending money, playing women, abusing women, and treating women as less than human. The "lucky" women in this video are just things—toys and scenery—not people.

The women in Jay-Z's video and in countless other pop culture images are objects for someone else's enjoyment. They are not presented as human beings with their own interests and desires. One theme in pop culture is that men are dominant, with positions of power. Women are

Guerilla Girls formed in 1985 to protest the underrepresentation of works by women in the art world. In this poster from 1989, the group highlights the degree to which women are presented naked in works of art. In public, members wear guerrilla masks to keep the focus on the issues and off who they might be as individuals.

submissive and subordinate (less important than men). Binary gender norms see gender nonconforming people negatively. Trans women are seen as rejecting masculinity (considered good) and choosing femininity (considered bad). So in many comedy films, including *White Chicks, Zoolander 2,* and *Deadpool,* trans women and men dressing up like women are played for laughs. They are always the butt of the joke.

Objectification and degradation of women influence how men view women. They also influence how women view themselves. For example, many girls and women try to achieve white, Eurocentric standards of beauty. They work hard to make themselves objects of desire. In this way, they internalize the belief that the most important thing about a woman is her attractiveness to men. Sometimes women police the behavior and appearance of other women. One way they do this is through bullying.

Marika Tiggemann is a professor of psychology and social work at Flinders University in Adelaide, Australia. In 2001 she reviewed the research on the effects of objectification on women's mental health. She found that objectification increases shame and anxiety about body image. This puts women at risk for eating disorders and depression. Caroline Heldman is the research director for the Geena Davis Institute on Gender in Media in Los Angeles, California. Heldman says, "Pop culture sells women and girls a hurtful lie: that their value lies in how sexy they appear to others, and they learn at a very young age that their sexuality is for others."

What does this have to do with the way women experience sexual harassment and assault? Javacia Harris is the founder and president of See Jane Write based in Birmingham, Alabama. She says, "Portraying a woman's body and sexuality as merchandise, as entertainment, is more than disrespectful. It's dangerous, because it becomes much easier to demand, even force, a woman to give you her body once she's been transformed from a person into property." This process is called dehumanization (failing to recognize the humanity of another person).

Object or Human?

Pop culture is bursting with pictures of the idealized female body depicted in magazines, advertisements, videos, and movies. How can we separate images that celebrate and empower from those that objectify? Caroline Heldman suggests using a series of questions to better understand and judge images we encounter in daily life:

- Does the image show isolated and sexualized parts of a human body, such as cleavage or a woman's hip?
- Does the image present a sexualized person as a stand-in for an object like a beer bottle or perfume?
- Does the image show sexualized persons as interchangeable? For example, does it depict a series of images showing sexualized women who all look very similar?
- Does the image depict violence as sexy, like a high-fashion ad that shows a man holding a woman down and pulling off her clothing?
- Does the image suggest that sexual availability is the most important characteristic of the person?
- Does the image show a sexualized person as a commodity that can be bought and sold?
- Does the image depict the human body as a surface used to display a product for advertising? For example, does the ad use a woman's body as a table to hold the items that are for sale?

In 2015 Madame Tussauds wax museum in Las Vegas, Nevada, added a wax figure of mega pop star Nicki Minaj on all fours. The figure is based on her character in the popular music video "Anaconda." Some critics point to Minaj's exposed buttocks and posture as an example of the objectification of black women. Do you think the wax figure is an example of objectification? Or does it present Minaj as an empowered woman?

CROP TOPS AND LOW-RISE JEANS

When Willa started high school, the teachers at her school presented the dress code through a skit to assembled students. She describes it, saying, "There was this one guy on the stage accompanied by about three girls. I remember clearly that one of the girls dressed in a tank top and bent over so her cleavage was on display, and said in a flirty voice, 'Hi! Good morning, Mr. Davis!' to the guy (playing 'Mr. Davis') who then 'acted' all uncomfortable and distracted. . . . What was this demonstration really saying? That girls should be objectified by their teachers? Or girls better cover up or they might get objectified by their teachers?"

Girls at schools across the United States have been sent home for everything from bare arms to exposed bra straps. In 2017 Kelsey Paige Anderson, a seventeen-year-old student at Joplin High School in Missouri wore jeans and a long-sleeved peasant blouse to class. In front of other students, her teacher told Kelsey that she was too busty and plus-sized for the outfit and merited a dress code violation.

The dress codes at many schools focus on what girls wear and how they look. Girls are told that they can't wear anything revealing that might distract boys from their studies. One underlying meaning seems to be that female bodies are shameful and should be covered up. Another meaning is that we shouldn't expect straight boys to be able to control their sexual urges around female bodies. In the context of rape culture, one-sided dress codes excuse sexual harassment. They imply that the sight of a woman's collarbone or the curve of her hip makes it impossible for a man to stop himself from reaching out and grabbing her flesh.

Not only do school dress codes tend to focus on the appearance of girls, but also girls are dress-coded far more often than boys. This creates a double standard in which there are different and unbalanced rules for girls. High schooler Madeline Bruce describes her experience of the dress code double standard. She says, "I lived in fear of being

In 2017 Molly Neuner, a sixth grader at King Middle School in Portland, Maine, protested the school's dress code, arguing that it was sexist and unfairly targeted girls. She was spurred into action after one of her teachers shamed her in front of her class for wearing a workout tank top to school. Neuner brought the issue to the attention of the school's administration. The school superintendent agreed to work with Neuner and others to rethink the entire school district's dress code.

disciplined for my clothing. Boys could get away with wearing shirts with women in bikinis on them, yet girls couldn't show their bra straps without being called out. Boys could wear cutoffs, but girls couldn't wear shorts that were 'fingertip length' standing up, but not sitting down. Boys could take their shirts off during band rehearsal, but girls were disciplined for wearing spandex shorts and sports bras during the same rehearsal. The double standard of my school dress code showed itself to me, and I was furious."

WHITE BLOSSOMS AND DEFLOWERED STEMS

The popular television show *Jane the Virgin* launched in 2014. In the very beginning of the first season, Jane's grandmother tells Jane that her virginity is like an unblemished flower. If you crush the blossom in your hand, you can never make it fresh again. The same message is offered by many abstinence-only sex education programs. In these programs, the focus is on saying no to sex outside of marriage. In one popular curriculum, the instructor emphasizes the message by passing

Check the Code

In May 2015, a group of middle-school students in Oregon went to a school board meeting in their town to protest dress code policies. They believed that the rules discriminated against female students. They felt that the rules were a form of public shaming and cost girls too much in missed class time. One of the students, eighth-grader Sophia Carlson, told the board, "Since only female students received dress code violations on the basis that what they were wearing was distracting to boys, it taught male students that it is acceptable to misbehave and disrespect women if their skin is showing, and it taught female students that making sure male students had a distraction-free learning environment is more important than her own education."

The students' activism and the work of members of Oregon NOW (the Oregon chapter of the National Organization for Women) led to change. The school district—Oregon's largest—wrote a new and gender-neutral dress code. The rules apply equally to all students. The complete code is at https://www.pps.net/Page/7980. Below are some of the key points:

- Students must wear clothing including both a shirt and pants or skirt, or the equivalent, and shoes.
- Shirts and dresses must have fabric in the front and on the sides.
- Clothing must cover undergarments, waistbands, and bra straps excluded.
- Fabric covering all private parts must not be see-through.
- Clothing may not depict pornography, nudity, or sexual acts.
- Clothing may not use or depict hate speech targeting groups based on race, ethnicity, gender, sexual orientation, gender identity, religious affiliation, or any other protected groups.

a rose around the room, telling each student to pull off a petal. When the damaged flower has made the rounds, the instructor announces that the flower represents a girl who has had casual sex. She is now ugly, unwanted, and used up.

What about her sexual partners? Are they deflowered stems too?

In the United States, girls and boys receive very mixed messages about sexual behavior. Girls are depicted as flowers whose beauty is valued and whose purity needs to be guarded at all costs. Boys are presented as sexually voracious animals who can't be expected to control their "natural" urges. In a rape culture, sex becomes a battlefield. On one side is the army of toxic masculinity driven by unruly hormones. The army's goal is to break through a girl's defenses and take the prize—sex. On the other side is the army of girls and women. They are supposed to be gatekeepers, keeping the army of boys and men at bay. In rape culture, men are not responsible for their sexual actions. Women are the ones who must ward off male aggression. Because of this skewed view of sex, if a woman is raped, she is often blamed for failing to resist.

#YESALLWOMEN

Consider this scenario: A woman has gone out dancing with some friends. A guy, also hanging out with his friends, asks if she wants to dance. She declines and goes back to her friends. He moves closer and tells her she's hot. She tries again to turn him down. This time, he gets angry, demanding to know why she wore that short skirt if she doesn't want the attention. She avoids the question. He pesters her. "Do you have a boyfriend? Are you a lesbian? What's wrong with you?" She tells him that she just wants to hang with her friends. He gets angry and calls her a foul name. Finally, the woman and her friends decide to leave. Their night has been ruined by a pushy guy who wouldn't take no for an answer.

Scenarios like this are common in public spaces that girls and women

> "Women are rarely taught how to say yes to sex, or how to act out their own desires. Rather, we are told that the rules of sexual engagement involve men pushing and women putting on the brakes."
>
> —Jill Filipovic, journalist, *Yes Means Yes*, 2008

inhabit. This hypothetical scene illustrates a phenomenon called male sexual entitlement. This is the belief that men can behave as if they have a right to attention from women and to access to their bodies. An extreme example of male sexual entitlement occurred in Isla Vista, California, in the spring of 2014. That year a twenty-two-year-old man, enraged by what he saw as the failure of women to appreciate him, went on a shooting rampage. He killed six people and injured fourteen more in an attack that specifically targeted a sorority house at the University of California, Santa Barbara.

Afterward, investigators found that the shooter, who killed himself after the attack, had left behind disturbing videos and a 147-page manifesto (a statement of his motives and views). In some of the most disturbing material, he wrote, "I don't know why you girls aren't attracted to me, but I will punish you all for it. . . . You are animals and I will slaughter you like animals. And I will be a god." The Isla Vista killer was driven by misogyny and an extreme sense of male sexual entitlement. He believed he deserved sex from the women he desired. When they withheld it from him, his hatred grew. Investigators discovered that well before the murders, the killer had written about hitting on two young women. When they declined his advances, he became enraged and threw his coffee on them. He wrote, "How dare those girls snub me in such a fashion! How dare they insult me. . . . They deserved the punishment I gave them. It was such a pity that my latte wasn't hot enough to burn them. Those girls deserved to be dumped in boiling water for the crime of not giving me the attention and adoration I so rightfully deserve!"

After the shooting, @gildedspine, an American woman on Twitter, created the hashtag #YesAllWomen to capture women's everyday experiences with male sexual entitlement. The hashtag trended for several days. More than one million people all across the globe shared their stories on Twitter of sexism, harassment, assault, and rape. Like the 2017 #MeToo hashtag, #YesAllWomen demonstrated the frequency

Voices of #YesAllWomen

I am a rape and sexual assault survivor and my experience is not particularly unusual or rare. #YesAllWomen

[Violence against women is common] because we teach girls to dress decent instead of teaching boys to act decent. #YesAllWomen

Learning to say "I have a boyfriend" is the easiest way to get a man to leave you alone. Because he respects another man more than you. #YesAllWomen

[Rape is perpetuated] because society is more comfortable with people telling jokes about rape than it is with people revealing they've been raped. #YesAllWomen

Every single woman you know has been harassed. And just as importantly, every single woman you don't know has been harassed. #YesAllWomen

[Injustice prevails] because the media will mourn the lives of ruined high school football players, but not of the girls they assault. #YesAllWomen

I shouldn't have to hold my car keys in hand like a weapon and check over my shoulder every few seconds when I walk at night. #YesAllWomen

of negative, demeaning, and sometimes violent interactions women have with men in person and online. In a twist of horrific irony, many of the responses from men to women who wrote posts tagged with #YesAllWomen included threats of rape and murder.

SMEAR CAMPAIGN

Male sexual entitlement means that saying no to sex can be dangerous and even deadly for women.

What about when women say yes? That often doesn't go well either. As with dress codes, there are double standards when it comes to sex. Sixteen-year-old Max describes it this way: "My friend Nick's ex-girlfriend, Amy, recently complained to me about rumors Nick had started about her. At first I sort of shrugged and had a *what can you do?* attitude. This changed when I realized he was calling her a slut because she hooked up with a guy at a party after Nick broke up with her. This was completely absurd (and blatantly sexist) because he and I were at that same party and we both hooked up with more than two girls each, and we got nothing but praise from our friends."

What happened to Amy is slut shaming. It means using words like *slut* or *skank* to put down and denigrate girls for their appearance, their attitudes about sex, or their sexual behavior. These slurs suggest promiscuity even if the girl is not sexually active and imply that the girl has something to be ashamed of. Boys are rarely the targets of slut shaming. That's because society has rules for boys and their sexual behavior that are much looser than the rules for girls. Boys are expected to be interested in sex. People generally think it's great when a boy pursues sex with enthusiasm. However, society expects girls to be more cautious and less eager to have sex than boys. So if a girl is not ashamed of her body nor of her sexuality, people tend to be critical of her.

Slut shaming isn't really about a girl's actual attitude about sex or about her behaviors. It's about power. Sex columnist JR Thorpe says, "The idea of a slut is just patriarchal, female-sexuality-policing drivel designed to be an all-purpose female putdown." When a boy accuses a girl of being a slut, it's a way for the boy to say he is in control of who and what that girl is. He has power over her.

Race and class intersect with gender, so slut shaming is also a way for white women to have power over women from marginalized groups. Sociology professors Elizabeth Armstrong and Laura Hamilton studied slut shaming among women at Midwest University in Wentzville, Missouri. They found that women often used accusations of promiscuity to smear women they didn't like, regardless of actual sexual behavior. The researchers found that rich women thought poor

Take Down the Shamers

Sex columnist JR Thorpe offers some excellent comebacks if you or someone else is being slut-shamed:

- Instead of trying to convince the bully that you're not what they say you are, shut down the shamer with "My body, my rules."
- React with a question that throws the judgment back on the judger: "Why does this bother you so much?"
- Support someone who is being slut-shamed by validating their appearance and actions: "I think you're slaying it."
- Stand up for a friend by asking the bully to stay in their lane: "What does her sexual behavior have to do with you?"

women were sluts and vice versa. However, only poor women were called out as sluts in public. "The high-status women would literally snub or look through the poorer women," said Armstrong. "If you want to make a young woman feel bad, pulling out the term 'slut' is a surefire way to do it. . . . It's [a way to say] 'she isn't one of us, we don't like her and she's different.'"

Slut shaming is far from innocent. Like other forms of bullying, slut shaming deeply impacts women and girls. Many targets end up feeling worthless and hopeless. Some experience negative body image, eating disorders, depression, anxiety, and self-harming behaviors. In extreme cases, some girls may feel they have no escape from the toxic environment created by slut shaming. In desperation they may take their own lives.

GET A GOOD CAMERA ANGLE

We receive messages about personal identity, gender roles, intimate relationships, and sexuality in many ways. They come from our families, our communities, the people we hang out with in school, pop culture, and the media. The messages are diverse, messy, complicated, and often contradictory. When women express their sexuality, the way they do it is often hotly debated. Is the woman objectified, or is she empowered?

Kim Kardashian, famous for being famous, posts many selfies to her fifty-nine million followers. Often she is either naked or nearly naked. She says that good camera angles are essential for her nude photos. And she comments, "I think I have the control to put out what I want and I'm proud of that. So even if I'm objectifying myself, I feel good about it." When the internet blew up over a nude picture she put on Instagram in March 2016, Kardashian responded by saying, "I am empowered by my body. I am empowered by my sexuality. I am empowered by feeling comfortable in my skin. I am empowered by showing the world my flaws and not being afraid of what anyone is going to say about me."

Kardashian is using language that in some ways suggests she agrees with one of feminism's key philosophies—that women should be in charge of their own bodies, their own sexuality, and how they present themselves. When Kardashian posts nude selfies, is she in charge? Melissa Fabello, the comanaging editor of the online magazine *Everyday Feminism*, isn't so sure. She says, "If the sexuality being sold by the media is one that subjugates [dominates] women and pushes willing objectification off as sexual ownership, then when we buy into and mirror it, are we really experiencing liberation?"

Conversation with female friends about dating. I said I liked dating, even bad dates, because dating can be a kind of adventure. Worst case, you learn something about yourself. Female friend said something like, 'No, worst case is I'm raped and killed.' That's when I got it."

—Andy Khouri, DC Comics editor, on Twitter, 2018

Body Strong

Psychologist Caroline Heldman suggests four ways to fight back against sexual objectification:

- Enjoy your body as a powerful, competent physical instrument. Run, climb, dance, parkour, or skateboard—do whatever makes you feel strong.
- Do something "embarrassing" every day. You exist for you. Skip in public. Talk about your period. Be goofy. Don't worry about making other people uncomfortable.
- Worry less about what you look like, and spend your time doing meaningful things. Learn a language. Try a new sport. Spend time with good friends. Give back to your community. You do you.
- Give yourself love and compassion. Let go of putting yourself and your body down. You are enough.

Rock climbing indoors or out is a great way to enjoy the strength of the human body. It's also a great way to say no to sexual objectification.

The key to separating objectification from empowerment is power. As illustrator Ronnie Ritchie points out in a comic called *Who Has the Power?*, "If the person who is being 'looked at,' or sexualized, has the power in the situation, then they are sexually empowered."

Fabello puts it this way: "Sexual empowerment is active. It's ownership. Autonomous. Self-serving. Objectification, on the other hand, is a passive relenting [giving up] of control. It's powerless. Self-sacrificial."

In the case of Kim Kardashian, her wealth and fame give her a lot of power. She's not pressured into appearing naked. But she's also participating in the message that a woman's worth is defined by her sexual appeal. And what about a teen who is getting pressured by a guy in her class to post a nude selfie? She might decide to do it and feel sexy about doing it. But it wasn't really her idea, so she's not controlling the situation. It can turn ugly if the guy decides to spread the image publicly or use it to control her.

CHAPTER FIVE
I NEED YOU TO BELIEVE ME

Police officer #1 to rape survivor: Tell us what happened.

Rape survivor: I didn't drink much. I can show you my bank account, how many drinks I had. The last thing I remember is being with friends in a bar. I woke up and a man I don't know was having sex with me, unprotected. . . . When I left the apartment, a man followed me. . . . He insisted on sharing a cab . . . and told me we'd had sex the night before. I went home and changed my shirt and got to work two hours late and then left early and came here [to the police station].

Police officer #2: Why did you share a cab? Why did you leave the bar with a stranger? Why didn't you call the police this morning?

Rape survivor: I don't know, I was confused—I never have [been raped] before. I was scared of exactly this [being grilled by the police].

Police officer #2: You must admit, it's odd that you went to work if you actually thought you'd been raped.

FALSE REPORTS ARE RARE

In this real-life exchange, the victim is scared and confused. The questions asked by the police officers suggest that they don't believe she was really raped. The statistics suggest that they should believe her. On average, 321,500 people in the United States are sexually assaulted every year. Yet according to the 2013 National Crime Victimization Survey, only 36 percent of rapes are reported to the police. Of those reports, only 12 percent lead to arrest and even fewer to conviction. The vast majority of rapists in the United States face no consequences for their crimes. They are free to rape again, and most rapists are serial offenders who make a habit of raping people.

Why don't rape survivors report the crimes committed against them?

If the rapist was a classmate or coworker, some might fear retribution at school or work. Women of color and immigrant women might not want to focus the attention of law enforcement on their communities, which are frequently targets of police violence. Other

Police interrogations are often portrayed in movies and on TV as friendly exchanges between a victim and law enforcement agents. This is especially true if the woman fits the stereotypical profile of the "perfect victim"—white, wealthy, sweet, and virginal. In reality, the interviews can be harsh and may focus the blame on the victim herself. In this still from the 1944 movie classic *Laura*, Dana Andrews as Detective Mark McPherson questions Laura (played by Gene Tierney) about a murder in which she is implicated.

survivors might want to put the experience behind them and try to move on. Still others might fear that friends, family, and authorities won't believe them. Consider the real-life experience of the police grilling the rape survivor. She told them that she woke up with a stranger's penis inside her. This is, by definition, a rape. Yet the second officer clearly doubted her account. Instead of asking her why she went to work after the rape, the officer suggested she perhaps had not been raped. He did so by saying to her that she only "thought" she'd been raped, instead of saying "after you'd been raped." The officer didn't believe the rape survivor. And he's not the only one who doesn't believe survivors.

In the 1990s, members of the sex crimes unit of the police department in Philadelphia, Pennsylvania—the officers and detectives who investigate sexual assault and rape—nicknamed their division the "lying bitch unit." Another officer, in the sex crimes unit of the police department in Baltimore, Maryland, said, "In homicide, there are real victims; all our [rape] cases are bullshit."

In 2010 sociologist Amy Dellinger Page at Appalachian State University in Boone, North Carolina, evaluated officers from eleven police and sheriff's departments. She measured their acceptance of common rape myths. More than 20 percent agreed with the statement "Women falsely report rape to call attention to themselves." From 2004 to 2006, sociologist Martin D. Schwartz was a visiting research fellow at the National Institute of Justice in Washington, DC. He asked 428 first responders this question: "What percentage of rape reports do you think (your gut feeling) never happened; they are false reports?" Almost one-third of the respondents believed that the false reporting rate was over 50 percent. Some respondents said the rate was closer to 95 or 100 percent. In other words, some of these police officers thought that all women lie about rape.

These beliefs are completely false. In fact, according to research conducted by David Lisak, the actual rate of false reports of sexual assault in the United States each year is between 2 and 8 percent. Out of one hundred women who say they've been raped, almost every single one is telling the truth.

WHY DON'T WE BELIEVE RAPE SURVIVORS?

The short answer is that we don't want to.

Rape culture tells a very specific—and false—story about what rape is and who commits it. The story goes like this: A deviant and violent stranger snatches a sweet and virginal woman from the street at random. She screams and fights as he brutally assaults her and leaves her for dead, covered in bruises and bleeding from her injuries. The reality is that very few rapes follow this script. Most rapists are not strangers. Seven out of ten of them know their victims, who can be from any walk of life—people of color, disabled people, LGBTQ+, poor people, or sex workers. Many rapes leave very little physical damage on victims.

When an attack doesn't follow the "stranger danger" model, people are baffled. Friends, coworkers, police, medical professionals, members of the legal system, and even family members would rather believe that a victim is lying than that an assault has occurred. They use common myths—even cultural lies—about rape and rapists to justify their denial.

He's a nice guy. She must be lying. Dr. Larry Nassar was one of the so-called nice guys. He was a well-educated, highly respected, married white man who was the medical coordinator for USA Gymnastics and an associate professor in the College of Osteopathic Medicine at Michigan State University. As an osteopathic physician, Nassar treated physical aches and pains by using stretching, massagelike pressure, and physical adjustments to bring relief to tight muscles and joints. He had built a reputation as a person who could help elite athletes reach their highest potential. According to Jade Capua, a former gymnast, she was advised to see Nassar because "he's a miracle worker. He can fix anyone or anything." Parents considered themselves lucky to get their young athletes into his care. They believed he had the power to make or break an athlete's career in the elite circles of Olympic sports.

In reality, Nassar sexually assaulted hundreds of girls, including Capua. One victim, Kyle Stephens, was six years old when the abuse began. When she was twelve, she told her parents. They accused her of lying. They chose to believe Nassar, a close family friend and a *nice guy*. Stephens's father even made her apologize to Nassar for making the accusations.

Some parents were in the examination room when Nassar assaulted their daughters. He inserted his fingers into their vaginas and anuses during what were supposed to be routine medical treatments. Kristen Chatman said that when she took her daughter, Chloe Myers, for treatment, she "was fully covered—even wearing running shorts. I, unlike others, don't remember him 'blocking' my view, but since she was covered, I was unaware of what he was doing under the sheet. After

Former Michigan State University and USA Gymnastics doctor Larry Nassar (*foreground*) went to trial in Lansing, Michigan, in 2017. He was accused of molesting dozens of female athletes over several decades. He pleaded guilty to multiple counts of criminal sexual conduct. In early 2018, he was sentenced to 40 to 175 years in prison for his crimes.

he was done, he washed his hands and I remember thinking 'Did he just do what I think he did? Where are his gloves?' I immediately dismissed the thoughts as there must have been some good reason. This was Larry after all. No need to question him. . . . We all trusted him."

At Nassar's trial in January 2017, the judge made time for more than 150 of the women whom Nassar had assaulted, including many Olympic gymnasts, to speak out. In their impact statements, they talked about the effect his sexual predation had had on their lives. Nassar sat in the courtroom as woman after woman recounted the effects of his abuse, including sleeplessness, nightmares, depression, anxiety, and suicide attempts. Over and over again, these survivors pointed out that Nassar's reputation as a skilled doctor and a *nice guy* were used to shield him at their expense. In January 2018, Nassar was sentenced to 40 to 175 years in prison for his crimes. In May of the same year, Michigan State University, whose officials had covered up Nassar's abuses, agreed to pay a $500 million settlement to his victims.

It wasn't really rape. She must be lying. The victim says it was rape. The perpetrator says it was consensual. People who side with the perpetrator offer a variety of excuses for the rapist. The victim probably consented but was too drunk to remember. She probably regretted the sex and decided to make a false accusation so she wouldn't look bad. She's a slut, and sluts can't get raped. She probably lied to get attention.

Jamie Dantzscher was one of the Olympic gymnasts who testified in court against Nassar. About her testimony, she said, "I was attacked on social media. . . . People didn't believe me, even people I thought were my friends. They called me a liar, a whore, and even accused me of making all of this up just to get attention." Amanda Thomshow, a student at Michigan State University, was raped by Nassar during a medical examination. She said, "I reported it. Michigan State University, the school I loved and trusted, had the audacity to tell me that I did not understand the difference between sexual assault and a medical procedure." This is a form of gaslighting (a manipulative attempt to make someone doubt the reality of an experience). Gaslighting deeply traumatizes victims. Long-term manipulation can make it impossible for some victims to see the difference between assault and healthy sexuality.

Jamie Dantzscher is an Olympic Games gymnastics bronze medalist—and a survivor of sexual abuse at the hands of Dr. Larry Nasser. In March 2017, Dantzscher testified before the US Senate Judiciary Committee hearing about protecting young athletes from sexual abuse.

Black Girls: Adultified and Sexualized

In 2017 the Georgetown Center on Poverty and Inequality, based in Washington, DC, did a survey to learn more about how adults view black girls. The results showed that adults tend to "adultify" black girls, perceiving them "as less innocent and more adult-like than white girls of the same age." Kimberly Springer, the curator for oral history at Columbia University in New York, explains that black girls and women are also hypersexualized, meaning they are often viewed as more promiscuous than white women. These false beliefs come from the same racist attitudes that present black men as automatic sexual threats to the purity of white women. Black women are seen as sexually aggressive, so if a black woman is raped, she is often portrayed as a "slut" who was "asking for it." Springer says this is a common view. Throughout the history of the United States, the myth of the hypersexualized black woman "served to set white women on a pedestal [of sexual purity] and excuse white men's rape of black women. If black women were [in this myth] always ready and willing sexual partners, it was impossible to have sex with them against their will." Society and the legal system—with this legacy of racism—often fail to take the sexual assault of black girls and women as seriously as that of white girls and women.

She was asking for it. She must be lying. What were you wearing? Why did you go to that party? Were you flirting? Are you sexually active? Had you had sex with him before? Did you try to fight him off? Often survivors are asked questions like these that imply they are to blame for their assault. Authorities, friends, family members, and the community at large are most likely to believe—though not always—young, white, pretty, sober, virginal victims who typically wear modest clothing. By contrast, society is more likely to say that people of color or those who are not beautiful, not sober, or not virginal—and who wear so-called immodest clothing—were *asking for it*. This victim blaming often goes hand in hand with slut shaming. Women who are sexually active or dress provocatively are often accused of inviting violation because they are "sluts." But as author and feminist Kate Harding explains, "It is literally impossible to ask for rape. Rape, by definition, is sex you did not ask for. So either you mean that a woman who dresses a certain way, or flirts, or otherwise expresses her sexuality on her own terms somehow *deserves* to be raped—which would make you a monster—or you are wrong, and she was not asking for it."

BEHIND A DUMPSTER

Late one night in January 2015, two Swedish graduate students were biking home through the campus of Stanford University in Palo Alto, California. Behind a dumpster near the Kappa Alpha fraternity house, they saw a young white man, later identified as Brock Turner, thrusting his hips into the body of an unresponsive white woman. When they stopped and called out to Turner, he tried to run away. The students chased after him. One tripped Turner. The other tackled him and held Turner down while his friend checked on the victim. She was alive, but extremely drunk and unresponsive. They restrained Turner until the police arrived and arrested him. He was later indicted (charged) on five different counts. Turner went to trial in March 2016 and on March 30 was found guilty of three felony charges. At his sentencing, "Emily Doe" (a pseudonym for the woman who survived the attack) read aloud to her rapist part of a powerful twelve-page impact statement she had written. Shortly after, she shared the entire letter with BuzzFeed News for publication. In part, she said,

> You don't know me, but you've been inside me, and that's why we're here today. . . . [When I first woke up in the hospital] all I was told was that I had been found behind a dumpster, potentially penetrated by a stranger. . . . I tried to push it out of my mind, but it was so heavy I didn't talk, I didn't eat, I didn't sleep, I didn't interact with anyone . . .
>
> [I learned from a newspaper article that] I was found unconscious, with my hair disheveled, long necklace wrapped

The Red Zone

Many campus administrators call the period from the first day of college in the fall until Thanksgiving break in November the Red Zone. That's the time of year when freshman students are most likely to be sexually assaulted. During the Red Zone, new college students suddenly have way more freedom than they are used to having. At the same time, they are plunged into social situations with lots of people they don't know, and they haven't yet had the chance to make new friends who will look out for them. Alcohol flows freely at parties, but some young people don't have a good sense of what their tolerance to alcohol will be. These conditions often lead to binge drinking in unfamiliar situations with unfamiliar people. This makes new students very vulnerable. Sexual predators know this and take advantage of it.

Navigating the Red Zone takes awareness. It means knowing that this period is especially risky. It means going to parties with people you trust. It means listening to your gut instincts when meeting new people. If you don't feel comfortable or safe with someone, don't be alone with them. And it means being extra careful about drugs and alcohol. Anyone who is drunk or high is less able to stay safe and to advocate for themselves and others. In a rape culture, girls and women must take precautions such as these.

around my neck, bra pulled out of my dress, dress pulled off over my shoulders and pulled above my waist, that I was butt naked all the way down to my boots, legs spread apart. . . . My breasts had been groped, fingers jabbed inside me along with pine needles and debris, my bare skin and head had been rubbing against the ground behind a dumpster, while an erect freshman was humping my half naked, unconscious body.

[During the trial] I was pummeled with narrowed, pointed questions that dissected my personal life, love life, past life, family life, inane [silly] questions, accumulating trivial details to try and find an excuse for this guy who had me half naked before even bothering to ask for my name. . . . You took away my worth, my privacy, my energy, my time, my safety, my intimacy, my confidence, my own voice, until today.

Emily Doe was not a "perfect" victim, neither sober nor virginal. She had gone to a college fraternity party and had drunk to the point of blacking out. She already had a boyfriend, and she had been seen dancing and flirting with other men at the party. She couldn't remember anything about the rape. It was impossible for her to share her memories of what had happened. She didn't have any.

Turner's defense was that they had met at the party and that she had agreed to have sex with him. Many people believed this. They did not question that a woman would want to get intimate behind a garbage dumpster with a man she did not know. Others thought that by accusing Turner—a talented swimmer with Olympic dreams—of rape, she was trying to get attention. They claimed that women would actually want that kind of intense scrutiny of the most intimate details of their personal lives.

Turner was a very believable, so-called *nice guy*. He was wealthy, white, blond, blue-eyed, and good looking. He was a star athlete with a promising future. Leslie Rasmussen is one of Turner's childhood friends. At his sentencing, she vouched for Turner's character. She blamed the victim and the campus drinking culture for the assault:

Brock Turner fit the description of the average nice guy and was a talented competitive swimmer at Stanford University. For these reasons, many people excused the behavior for which he was accused, blaming his victim instead.

Let's Talk about Booze

The defense in the Brock Turner case claimed that because he was drunk, he shouldn't be held responsible for his actions. According to Turner's dad, Turner's character witness, and the judge, Turner was a good guy who drank too much and had a small lapse in judgment. It was the booze, not him. The victim's drunkenness was used to tell a totally different story. The defense depicted her as a stupid person who got so wasted at a party that she couldn't remember consenting to sex. Her inebriation made her unreliable, not believable, and unworthy of sympathy.

The contradictory approach to alcohol during Turner's trial highlights the way in which rape culture makes excuses for men at the expense of women. Patriarchy views men as good and worthy of mercy. Women are inferior and not worthy of compassion. Experts point out that being drunk is not an excuse for raping someone. Likewise, the drunken state of a woman does not give anyone a free pass to rape her. It's common for people to tell women that if they don't want to be raped, they shouldn't get drunk. But in a world without rape culture, a woman could drink too much, pass out at a party, and wake up the next day without having been assaulted.

Brock is not a monster. . . . I don't think it's fair to base the fate of the next [ten plus] years of his life on the decision of a girl who doesn't remember anything but the amount she drank to press charges against him. . . . Rape on campuses isn't always because people are rapists. It is because these universities market themselves as the biggest party schools in the country. . . . I am so sick of hearing that these young men are monsters when really, you are throwing barely 20-somethings into these camp-like university environments, supporting partying. . . . This is completely different from a woman getting kidnapped and raped as she is walking to her car in a parking lot. That is a rapist. These are not rapists. These are idiot boys and girls having too much to drink.

Turner, too, blamed alcohol and the campus drinking culture. He did not take responsibility for what he had done to his victim, focusing instead on himself. In a written statement to the judge prior to sentencing, Turner wrote, "I've been shattered by the party culture and risk-taking behavior that I briefly experienced in my four months at school. I've lost my chance to swim in the Olympics. I've lost my ability to obtain a Stanford degree. I've lost employment opportunity, my reputation and most of all, my life. These things force me to never want to put myself in a position where I have to sacrifice everything."

Turner saw himself, not the woman he raped, as the victim. His father, Dan Turner, echoed that view, saying, "[Brock's] life will never be the one that he dreamed about and worked so hard to achieve. That is a steep price to pay for 20 minutes of action out of his 20-plus years of life." Turner's "20 minutes of action" devastated the life of his victim. In her impact statement, she wrote, "I can't sleep alone at night without having a light on, like a five year old, because I have nightmares of being touched where I cannot wake up."

During Turner's trial, the defense pulled out all the familiar rape-culture lies:

> *Brock Turner is a nice guy. She must be lying.*
> *It wasn't really rape. She must be lying.*
> *She was asking for it. She must be lying.*

NOT ME, NOT YOU

Why do these myths about rape persist? Sociologists point to a deep human urge to feel safe. We don't want to accept that brothers, husbands, fathers, coworkers, supervisors, police officers, doctors, pastors, or teachers—any of the men we respect, care about, and love—can be sexual predators. If we convince ourselves that only deviant, bad guys commit rape, then we can feel safe with the rest of the men in our lives. Since we live in a patriarchal society, where men do have power over women, we'd rather feel safe with this societal reality

Joanne Smith founded Girls for Gender Equity in Brooklyn, New York, in 2000. Among the group's goals is to work with students to change the culture of sexual harassment in schools so they can learn in a safe environment. The organization also works to empower girls by tackling issues such as sexism, racial inequality, homophobia, and transphobia.

instead of scared. Kate Harding says, "This [the belief that men in our lives can't be rapists] is the myth that props up most of the other [rape myths]." But reality looks different. In fact, sexual predators can be any profession or role, any ethnicity, any religion, any gender, or any class. This doesn't mean all men are predators. It means that no single characteristic such as race, wealth, marital status, job title, or niceness accurately profiles who will be a sexual predator. It does mean, though, that most perpetrators are not strangers. Seven out of ten rapists are people the victim knows—acquaintances, colleagues, friends, current or former partners, and family members.

Victim blaming is another way to create an illusion of safety. Girls and women are often just as likely as men to blame female victims. Why wouldn't women empathize with other women? Joanne Smith is the founder of Girls for Gender Equity. She met with a group of middle-school girls after one of their classmates was assaulted. They shared observations such as "She was easy" and "She deserved it." These comments show that the girls saw the assault from the perpetrator's point of view rather than through the eyes of the victim. Smith says, "Blaming the victim by identifying with the aggressor allowed the girls to distance themselves from her, thereby creating a false sense of security."

What Were You Wearing?

In March 2014, Christine Fox saw a tweet from a man that read, "Nobody deserves to be raped. But you also shouldn't dress like a ho." She remembered her own rape. She remembered what she had been wearing—jeans, a tank top, and a pair of heels. Was it her fault she'd been raped because she went to the perpetrator's house? Because she accepted the drink he offered that was spiked with a date rape drug? Because of what she wore? She shared her thoughts on Twitter. Before long, hundreds of women and some men were tweeting what they had been wearing when they were raped.

The question—*What were you wearing?*—is not as innocent as it sounds. The question implies that the victim was raped because of what the victim was wearing. It's a form of victim blaming. *Were you dressed like a ho?* implies that if the victim was not dressed modestly, then the victim was asking to be raped.

Mary Simmerling, an assistant professor of public health at Weill Cornell Medical College in New York, wrote a poem that described what she was wearing when she was raped: a cotton T-shirt, a denim skirt, and white sneakers. In the poem, she wonders why anyone would think ending rape was as simple as changing clothes. She tells readers that she remembers what her rapist was wearing too, but no one seemed to care about that.

Simmerling's poem inspired Jen Brockman, the director of the Sexual Assault Prevention and Education Center at the University of Kansas in Lawrence, and Mary Wyandt-Hiebert, the director of Support, Training, Advocacy and Resources (STAR) Central, an education program at the University of Arkansas in Fayetteville about sexual assault and relationship violence. They created a visual art installation to show that a victim's outfit and sexual assault are unrelated. The project—called "What Were You Wearing?"—was unveiled at the University of Arkansas in the spring of 2014. It paired re-created outfits, mounted on the wall, with a description, written by the rape survivor who had worn it. What were the outfits? A red sweater and black skirt. A baggy orange shirt and loose pants. Pajamas. A child's pink-and-white striped dress.

Victim blaming comes from a common but false way of thinking called the just-world hypothesis. People want to believe that the world is fair and that people always get what they deserve. To justify this way of thinking, people make false assumptions about both positive and negative events. For example, if a person is a millionaire, then they must have worked hard to earn that money. On the other hand, if a person is sexually assaulted, it must be their fault because of what they wore or how much they drank or something they did.

Barbara Gilin is a professor of social work at Widener University in Chester, Pennsylvania. "Having worked with a lot of victims and people around them, [I know that] people blame victims so that they can continue to feel safe themselves," she explains. "I think it helps them feel like bad things will never happen to them. They can continue to feel safe. Surely, there was some reason that the neighbor's child was assaulted, and that will never happen to their child because that other parent must have been doing something wrong." Holding victims responsible for their misfortune is a psychological coping strategy. It allows people to avoid admitting that something just as unthinkable could happen to them. It also supports the fantasy that if we do everything "right," we will never be victims. But what if an assault happens anyway? Because of victim blaming, even the survivor might believe it was her fault.

THE JUDGE GOES EASY

Turner's case hinged on whether or not the jury believed the claim that the victim had consented to sex with Turner behind a dumpster. All members of the jury concluded that the victim was too incapacitated by alcohol to actively choose sexual interactions. They unanimously voted to convict Turner. But Judge Aaron Persky was troubled. At sentencing Persky said that he disagreed with the jury's decision. The judge believed Turner when he said that his victim had consented to sex. Persky thought that Turner's drunkenness made his behavior less bad than if he had been sober.

Sofie Karasek, a survivor of sexual assault, spoke at a 2016 protest in San Jose, California. Like many Californians, she was outraged by the six-month sentence Judge Aaron Persky handed down in the Brock Turner sexual assault conviction. Turner was released after serving half of his sentence and went on to appeal his conviction. Meanwhile, in 2018, Californians recalled Judge Persky.

Judge Persky decided to go easy on Turner. He pointed to Turner's potential for success, that he wasn't armed during the rape, and that he had no prior convictions. He felt a harsh sentence would unnecessarily devastate Turner's life. Persky sentenced Turner to only six months in county jail rather than the six years the victim's attorneys had requested. Turner served three months and was released on good behavior.

Many people who had followed the trial's progress were outraged that Persky contradicted the conclusions of the jury. Stanford University law professor Michele Dauber launched a recall campaign to remove Judge Persky from his elected judgeship. On June 5, 2018, voters in Santa Clara County voted 59 to 41 percent to recall him from office.

SIX MONTHS VS. FIFTEEN YEARS

Compare the Turner case to that of nineteen-year-old Cory Batey, a student at Vanderbilt University in Nashville, Tennessee. Like Turner, he was a handsome star athlete at an elite college. As in Turner's case, bystanders caught Batey in the act of sexually assaulting an unconscious white woman on the night of June 23, 2013. Like Turner, Batey was arrested, charged, and brought to trial. Yet unlike Turner, Batey was sentenced to fifteen years in prison.

Six months versus fifteen years. Why the difference? Laws in Tennessee, where Batey faced trial, are different from laws in California, where Turner's case went to court. But that explains only part of the inequality. The whole answer lies at the intersection of racism, sexism, and other forms of oppression. Brock Turner is white.

Cory Batey was charged with raping an unconscious female student in her dorm at Vanderbilt University in June 2013. Unlike Brock Turner, a white student who was let off with a very light sentence, Batey and another football player were found guilty on multiple counts of aggravated rape and sexual battery. Batey was sentenced to fifteen years in prison. Many critics point to race as the distinguishing factor between the vastly differing prison terms.

Cory Batey is black. Generally speaking, the criminal justice system treats people of color more harshly than white defendants. According to a 2017 study by the United States Sentencing Commission, black men convicted of crimes receive sentences that are on average 19.1 percent longer than those received by white men convicted of similar crimes.

In addition, people of color are much more likely to be wrongfully convicted of violent crimes, especially sexual assault. In cases where a black man is accused of raping a white woman, more than half result in false convictions. This miscarriage of justice is, in part, the legacy of white supremacy (the belief that white people are superior to people of color). It is also tied to racist attitudes about sexuality. Black men are often seen as a sexual threat to the purity of white women, and historically, the perceived threat was often punished with death.

In 1955 a group of white men in Mississippi kidnapped, tortured, and murdered fourteen-year-old Emmett Till (*left*) for allegedly flirting with a white woman. During the men's trial, Carolyn Bryant Donham claimed Till had groped her and made sexually crude comments. In the minds of many Americans. Till's alleged actions justified his murder. Donham admitted in 2008 that she had lied about the encounter. The US Department of Justice reopened the case in July 2018 based on that information.

White supremacist policies outlawed interracial marriage across most of the United States until 1967. In that year, the US Supreme Court ruled in a case about the interracial marriage of Mildred and Richard Loving. The couple had married in Washington, DC, where interracial marriage was legal. They moved back to Virginia, where it was not. In the case, *Loving v. Virginia*, the Supreme Court held that all laws forbidding interracial marriage in the nation were unconstitutional. Yet even with this ruling in place, racist attitudes about the sexual deviance of black men are still common. These beliefs prop up the myth that most rapists are men of color. The myth says that these men deserve harsh sentences like the one Cory Batey is serving out, while white men like Brock Turner get off easy.

CHAPTER SIX

IN THE LEGAL SYSTEM

After being drugged by a stranger in a bar and being sexually penetrated while she was unconscious, a woman (whose name remains private) went to a hospital emergency room. There she requested a sexual assault forensic exam. Later, she wrote about the experience for other survivors who might have to go through the long and stressful process. "The lobby of the hospital emergency room is hexagonal and dim. I wait in line to see the intake clerk, walled in with safety glass for privacy. I'm here for a rape kit. . . . A small, soft nurse with short black hair and muted blue scrubs slowly fills out forms while I huddle on the bed in my dirty clothes. Her name is Nancy. I smell like a bar. I stare into the flecks on the drop-ceiling while she haltingly reads the instructions on the kit aloud.

"'Once I open this, we can't take it back,' she says blankly.

"I hesitate. . . . She looks at me, wooden. 'Should I open it?'"

Following an assault, survivors have to decide whether to come forward. Should they confide in a friend or a parent? Should they get help on campus? Should they go to the hospital? Should they file a police report? If they decide to go to the authorities, a lengthy legal process is set in motion. Many decision points arise along the way, and the survivor makes only a few of them. The rest are in the hands of individuals in the criminal justice system and in the broader community. These individuals include medical professionals, police investigators, the prosecuting and defense attorneys, judges and juries, and often the media. The myths of rape culture can and often do influence all of these individuals.

THE BODY IS A CRIME SCENE

A sexual assault forensic exam is a medical procedure that is performed by a specially trained medical professional at a hospital or other health facility. The professional is either a sexual assault nurse examiner or a sexual assault examiner. A federal law called the Violence Against Women Act requires all states to provide sexual assault forensic exams

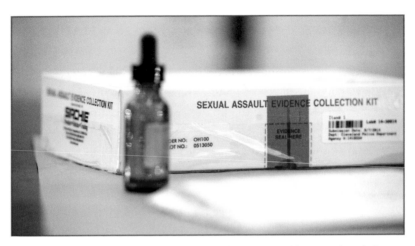

Sexual assault evidence kits, also called rape kits, contain evidence such as hair, blood, semen, and saliva. These samples are analyzed in forensic labs, and the genetic data are added to the Combined DNA Index System (CODIS).

at no cost to the survivor. When an adult survivor gets a sexual assault forensic exam, that person can choose whether to take the next step and go to the police. Either way, the exam provides and preserves crucial evidence in case the survivor decides to report the assault. For underage teens who have been sexually assaulted, the examiner may be required by mandatory reporting laws to report the assault to law enforcement.

The process is very detailed. First, the examiner offers immediate care for any injuries. Next, the examiner takes a detailed history about the survivor's general health, recent consensual sexual activity, and everything that happened during the assault. It's important for the survivor to give an accurate and complete account because it will guide the physical examination that comes next. The examiner documents (in writing or with photography) external damage to the body. This may include cuts and bruises and internal damage to the mouth, vagina, or anus. The examiner collects physical evidence such as hair, fabric fibers, semen, saliva, and blood in an evidence collection kit (often called a rape kit). Often the survivor's clothing, which may have evidence that can identify the perpetrator, will be saved for later forensic examination.

Getting a rape examination can take hours—long hours in a stark hospital room, long hours of poking and prodding and questions by stranger after stranger. For the survivor of an assault, this scrutiny can be an ordeal, a secondary trauma after the assault. Often the last thing a survivor wants to do is be exposed. Yet the rape kit is key to collecting critical evidence for a victim to pursue justice. The data from rape kits is often central to successful prosecution of sexual crimes. So even though a rape examination can be traumatizing, many victims want it done. They are motivated to stop the perpetrator from hurting anyone else. Many hospitals will connect survivors with a victim's advocate, a trained volunteer whose role is to support the survivor during and after a rape examination.

After the examiner has collected the samples and completed all the forms and documentation, the rape kit is sent to a police crime lab for analysis. Staff there creates a deoxyribonucleic acid (DNA)

Getting Help after an Assault

The Rape, Abuse & Incest National Violence Network (RAINN) is an organization dedicated to supporting survivors of sexual assault, preventing sexual violence, and improving criminal justice outcomes. RAINN operates a twenty-four-hour National Sexual Assault Hotline (800.656.HOPE). Many resources are available online (www.rainn.org), including how to get help after a sexual assault. Laws about sexual assault vary from state to state, so RAINN provides a searchable database with state-specific information about age of consent (related to statutory rape laws) and mandatory reporting requirements when minors are assaulted. It also has information about penalties for various forms of abuse and the statute of limitations (how long you can wait to report an assault) for sex crimes.

Crowded evidence rooms and lockers across the United States contain materials dating back many decades. Many cities have so many untested rape kits in storage they don't even keep a record of them. Without DNA evidence, a rape case is much harder to prosecute.

profile of the rapist from the genetic material in the kit. The profile is entered into a Federal Bureau of Investigation (FBI) database called the Combined DNA Index System (CODIS), where experts can compare it to other profiles. Matches in CODIS can identify suspects and can link the cases of multiple victims who have been assaulted by the same perpetrator. Most rapists are serial predators. They don't assault only one person. They commit sex crimes over and over again. Analyzing the sample from every single rape kit collected is very important. If this work isn't done, then many rapists will go undiscovered for years.

Yet hundreds of thousands of rape kits in the United States are stored—untested—in evidence lockers at police departments and in crime labs. There are so many of these kits—boxes full of blood samples and semen and hair and torn clothing—that many cities don't

Survivors Don't Have to Be Alone

Being the victim of a violent crime like sexual assault can be terrifying and confusing. The experience is traumatic. So is navigating the medical and legal systems. Survivors do not have to go through this alone. Victim's advocates are people who can accompany the survivor to medical procedures, explain the survivor's options for pursuing legal action, help the survivor fill out paperwork, be with the survivor in court, and offer nonjudgmental support at all stages. Some advocates are volunteers. Others work for hospitals, crisis centers, police departments, or county courthouses. RAINN and other local, nonprofit groups that support survivors of domestic and sexual assault can refer survivors to advocates.

Advocate and author Christa Desir says,

> To me, the most important thing for a rape crisis counselor or rape victim advocate is to listen to what a survivor needs and do everything possible to give the survivor her/his power back by offering information and resources and whatever else they need. . . . Advocates are necessary because they are the only ones in that space [hospitals, police stations, and attorneys' offices] whose primary objective is to empower the survivor. Advocates don't have an agenda to make them talk or tell their story or do the evidence collection kit or anything. Sometimes as an advocate, all I would do is sit and hold a survivor's hand, not asking anything of her beyond, "What can I help you with right now?"

even bother to keep an inventory of them. Nor do they perform genetic tests on the samples. In 2009 a prosecutor (an attorney who works to prove a suspect's guilt) decided to count and organize the rape kits stored in her department in Detroit, Michigan. She documented more than eleven thousand untested kits. That same year, twelve large US cities didn't have any idea how many untested kits they had in storage.

This is called the rape kit backlog, and it is a huge problem. Critical physical and genetic evidence often sits in a warehouse for years and even decades, untested and aging. DNA samples don't last forever.

From TV Star to Activist

In 1999 actor Mariska Hargitay earned the role of Detective Olivia Benson on *Law & Order: Special Victims Unit*. Since then she has starred in hundreds of episodes of this television crime procedural, which focuses primarily on sex crimes. During her career, many survivors of sexual assault have reached out to her and shared their experiences. As a result of these connections, Hargitay started the nonprofit Joyful Heart Foundation in 2004 to support survivors and work to end domestic and sexual violence.

One important initiative of the Joyful Heart Foundation is called End the Backlog. This program advocates for testing every single rape kit that is collected. The program works toward this goal in several ways. To get a scope of the problem, End the Backlog files public records requests on a city-by-city basis to learn how many untested rape kits exist. As of 2018, twenty-seven US cities had released their backlog data. Those cities had a total of thirty-nine thousand untested kits. Fourteen other US cities, including large cities such as Boston, Atlanta, and Baltimore, refused to release their information. Requests were pending in nineteen other cities. It seems likely that as many as one hundred thousand untested kits are in storage across the country. Each one represents an assault survivor who has not received justice.

Actor Mariska Hargitay founded the Joyful Heart Foundation. One of its goals is to end the rape kit backlog.

Another organization that works to eliminate the rape kit backlog in the United States is the Rape Kit Action Project. This organization advocates that states establish clear policies on rape kit testing requirements, track the number of untested kits, and create a plan to test all untested kits in the backlog.

The longer they sit, the harder it is to extract reliable information. DNA evidence is one of the most important tools authorities have to link rapists to their crimes. When rape kits remain untested, serial predators go free, and more innocent people are victimized.

If rape kits are so important to bringing rapists to justice, why are so many of them untested? If a crime has been committed, why is evidence ignored? The answers are varied and complex. They fall into these main categories:

Insufficient resources. Tracking rape kits, shipping them to crime labs, making sure they are processed, and putting the results into case files requires trained staff. Often law enforcement agencies don't have enough people to do the work. In addition, processing each kit costs $500 to $1,500. Many police departments have not prioritized using taxpayer dollars to pay for testing rape kits.

Lack of policies. As of 2018, only Connecticut, Illinois, Ohio, Michigan, Texas, Colorado, and New York had laws requiring the testing of all rape kits. Even with these laws in place, cities in these states may not have the money to do the testing. As a result, the decision to test a rape kit is made on a case-by-case basis. The choice depends heavily on police department attitudes toward sexual assault.

Bias and lack of training. Rape kits are more likely to be tested in police departments that prioritize sexual assault cases and understand that many rapists are serial predators. These departments are also more likely to have a sex crimes unit where staff is trained about the ways in which the false beliefs of rape culture create bias. A rape kit is most likely to be tested when police believe that victims are telling the truth.

WHEN POLICE ARE PART OF RAPE CULTURE

Studies have shown that the vast majority of rape survivors—92 to 98 percent—are telling the truth about the crimes committed against them. Yet many people in law enforcement assume that the victim is lying.

Black Women and Police Brutality

Many women from marginalized groups do not consider going to the police after a rape. They aren't sure the police will believe them. They may also fear further victimization. Black women make up 33 percent of women shot by the police. This is a high percentage because black women make up only 13 percent of the US population.

Policing in the United States emerged from slave patrols in the American South during the era when slavery was legal. Loosely organized patrol groups tracked and recaptured enslaved Africans who had escaped from white landowners. Recaptured people often faced brutal, sometimes deadly punishment. Even after slavery was abolished in the United States, black Americans endured devastating violence at the hands of law enforcement. For example, during the civil rights movement of the 1960s, police often broke up peaceful protests by black Americans using physical violence, tear gas, vicious police dogs, and power hoses. Black Americans are haunted by this history of violence, and many black Americans in the twenty-first century do not trust police officers. #BlackLivesMatter is a modern civil rights movement founded by Alicia Garza, Patrisse Cullors, and Opal Tometi in 2013. The movement draws attention to the disproportionate number of black people killed by police in the United States. An investigative report conducted by the *Washington Post* in 2016 showed that black people are 2.5 times more likely to be shot by police than are white people.

Death at the hands of police officers is only one threat that black

Twenty-eight-year-old Sandra Bland was found dead, hanging in her Texas jail cell, in 2015. She had been arrested during a routine traffic stop, and questions remain about whether she took her own life or was harmed while in police custody.

and other marginalized women face. Former Seattle police chief Norm Stamper says, "Sexual predation by police officers happens far more often than people in the business are willing to admit." An analysis by former officer Phil Stinson documented 548 cases of police sexual misconduct in the United States between 2005 and 2007. In 24 percent of these cases, the victims were minors. In other studies, data show that black women are stopped by police at a far higher rate than are white women. This puts them at higher risk of sexual assault by a police officer.

The hashtag #SayHerName was coined in 2015 to draw attention to the effects of police brutality on black women and trans women. It responded to the invisibility of black women among other social justice movements. For example, in a report from the African American Policy Forum in 2015, Kimberlé Crenshaw and police misconduct attorney Andrea Ritchie wrote, "Black women who are profiled, beaten, sexually assaulted, and killed by law enforcement officials are conspicuously absent from [Black Lives Matter] even when their experiences are identical [to those of black men]. When their experiences with police violence are distinct—uniquely informed by race, gender, gender identity, and sexual orientation—Black women remain invisible." #SayHerName memorializes women such as Rekia Boyd, Kayla Moore, Sandra Bland, and many others who were killed by police or died in police custody.

#SayHerName protesters gathered in New York in 2015 to call attention to black women who have died as a result of interactions with police.

This gap between reality and myth impacts the way rape cases are handled across the United States. If the police officer investigating a rape does not believe the victim, the officer will declare the case to be unfounded. The FBI defines an unfounded case as one that is "determined through investigation to be false or baseless." What if a case is unfounded simply because an officer, steeped in rape culture, decides with a shrug, "Eh, I just don't believe her?" The result would be that many victims would never see justice. In 2010 more than 30 percent of rape cases in Baltimore were declared to be unfounded. According to a 2014 investigation, the New Orleans, Saint Louis, and Philadelphia police departments purposely hid the actual number of reported rapes to avoid cases that are difficult to investigate and prosecute. They used three techniques: not creating any written documentation of rape accusations, unfounding cases without investigation, and reclassifying rape accusations to lesser crimes such as physical, not sexual, violence. They shelved rape kits and erased victims' stories.

The US Department of Justice focused a 2016 study on the Baltimore Police Department. The study found a systemwide failure to test rape kits. It also found widespread problems in the way police treat sexual assault victims. The report documented examples of officers mocking and insulting survivors. One officer called a survivor a "conniving little whore." Another demanded to know from the victim, "Why are you messing that guy's life up?" Officers sometimes revictimized survivors by strip-searching them in public. In some cases, officers offered to drive victims home and then raped them again. These are not things that happened only in Baltimore. Researchers have found similar situations in other places. For example, in the Missoula Police Department in Montana, police peppered survivors with victim-blaming questions such as, "Did you have an orgasm? Was this regret sex? Do you have a boyfriend?"

Writer, photographer, and child sex abuse survivor Elizabeth Tsung says, "These are circumstances due entirely to rape culture. If anyone says they were raped, we need to trust them and remind them it is never their fault. We need to abolish the fear of telling others, which is why so many cases of rape go unreported." Corey Rayburn Yung, a professor of law at the University of Kansas in Lawrence, adds, "Any success in decreasing sexual violence hinges on removing the numerous police-imposed obstacles inhibiting investigation and adjudication in rape cases [failure of officers to treat rape as a serious crime], beginning with substantial reform of police practices."

CENTERING VICTIMS

Human Rights Watch is an international, nonprofit organization that investigates and exposes abuses of power around the globe. In 2013 the group published a report on ways to improve police responses to sexual assault. The recommendations were based on research, including interviews with reform-seeking sex crime detectives and prosecutors, sexual assault nurse examiners, and rape victims' advocates. These are some of the main recommendations:

- The well-being of victims must always be at the center of any investigation. In the best departments, investigators begin with the assumption that the victim is telling the truth and that they have just experienced a significant trauma.
- Victims of trauma must be comforted and assured that they are safe.
- Victims must be allowed to tell their story in a nonjudgmental environment and in a comfortable space (not a cold, gray interrogation room).
- Officers must keep the interview focused on what happened during the assault.
- Well-trained officers know that experiencing trauma often leads to confused or contradictory memories.

- They also know that sex crimes create shame in victims, so victims might not offer details they think will paint them in a bad light. Neither fact means that the crime didn't occur.
- Officers must refer the victim to a victim's advocate and make them aware of available community resources for counseling and support.
- Officers must follow up with the victim as the investigation proceeds, to keep that person informed of case progress.
- Most importantly, anyone who works with a victim must treat that person as the victim of a violent crime—not as a criminal.

The Human Rights Watch report found that treating victims with kindness encourages them to cooperate with the legal system. Cooperation often leads to better outcomes in the long run. In other words, supporting the victim through the legal process increases the likelihood that the rapist will be brought to justice and gives the victim a smoother path toward healing.

IN THE COURTROOM

It's clear that bias within investigative departments can mean that not all rape reports are investigated properly and not all suspects are identified. If they are, the next step is for prosecutors to decide whether or not to pursue a legal case against a suspect. Prosecutors want justice served, but they also want to take cases that have a high probability of success. For a rape case, this means the existence of significant physical or genetic data that links a suspect to a victim and confirms that sexual contact occurred. Ideally, the victim has physical injuries. Ideally, the suspect looks like a criminal. In other words, the prosecutor wants a "perfect" victim, a deviant rapist, and a brutal assault. This is the most winnable case. But most rapes don't fit these criteria.

Why not? The suspect may be the victim's husband, a well-respected member of the community, or a police officer. The victim may be a sex worker, a drug addict, or a transgender person of color. Even if solid evidence proves a rape occurred, the prosecutor might not see a way to convince a jury to believe the victim over the suspect. In that situation, the prosecutor won't pursue the case. In 2004 Cassia Spohn, director of the School of Criminology and Criminal Justice at Arizona State University in Tucson, and David Holleran, associate professor at the College of New Jersey in Ewing, conducted a study. They looked at the prosecution of rape cases in Kansas City and Philadelphia. Even after a suspect had been arrested, only half of 526 cases actually went to court. That means that half of the arrested rape suspects—263 people—were released without consequences.

If a case does go to trial, rape myths catch fire in the courtroom. Defense attorneys have few restrictions on what they can do during a trial to challenge a victim's story. They often turn to strategies that play on the most common falsehoods about rape. They attack any part of the victim's life that will weaken her image as a perfect victim in the eyes of the jury. As Kate Harding puts it, "If you must be raped, you should try to be an upper-class white woman attacked by a poor person of color, because that's your best chance of being perceived as credible."

Unlike the judge at Brock Turner's trial, Judge Rosemarie Aquilina believed the victims who stood before her at Larry Nassar's trial. During the sentencing phase, she allowed every single survivor who wished to speak to do so. In a weeklong session of agonizing stories, more than 150 women read their impact statements. When Nassar protested that it was too painful for him to listen to the young women, Judge Aquilina told him, "You may find it harsh that you are here listening but nothing is as harsh as what your victims endured for thousands of hours at your hands, collectively. You spent thousands of hours perpetrating criminal sexual conduct on minors [people under

16 to 18 years old, depending on the state]. Spending four or five days listening to them is significantly minor considering the hours of pleasure you had at their expense and ruining their lives."

Legal Loopholes

When sexual assault occurs on a college campus, legal options for survivors can be murky. Often colleges and universities try to deal with harassment and assault "in house" instead of involving the local police jurisdiction. By doing so, schools avoid the bad publicity of a trial. But victims might not have access to the same level of legal protections as they would in the judicial system. With the in-house process, victims file an official complaint against the student who assaulted them. Both parties appear before a committee or panel of faculty (professors), staff, and sometimes other students. The group evaluates complaints made by one student against another. The people serving on these panels are as likely to be steeped in myths about rape as any member of the general population. Often their decisions do not favor victims. In many cases, victims are left with the difficult choice of either continuing to take classes with the person who assaulted them or dropping out of school.

Under President Barack Obama (in office from 2009 to 2017), the US government launched an effort to reduce sexual assault on college campuses. More thorough protections under Title IX required colleges and universities to do a better job of investigating allegations of assault. They also required schools to issue stricter penalties for perpetrators. In September 2017, Betsy DeVos, secretary of education for President Trump, canceled these guidelines. She said repeatedly during a speech that the rights of people accused of sexual harassment and abuse were being violated. Catherine Lhamon, an attorney and the former assistant secretary for civil rights in the US Department of Education, said, "The speech [by DeVos] pretty clearly sent a message that sexual assault will not be taken seriously by [the Trump] administration. That could not be more damaging."

CHANGING THE WAY WE TALK ABOUT RAPE

The media coverage of high-profile sexual assault trials often questions the believability of victims. It also bolsters rape culture by using language that blames the victim for her own assault. Discussions of sexual assault in regular conversations tend to do the same thing. Much of the language Americans use to discuss rape erases the rapist. For example, a person might say about a rape survivor, "She was raped" instead of "A man raped her." Well-meaning advice often goes along these lines: "This is how you protect yourself from being raped" instead of "Men shouldn't rape women." News coverage of intimate-partner violence claims that "violence against women is a problem" instead of that "men who commit violent crimes against women are the problem." Through language and the word choices people make, rape becomes something that happens to women, not something that men do. Jackson Katz is a filmmaker and cofounder of the Mentors in Violence Prevention program at Northeastern University in Boston. In his TED Talk, he says, "[It is] amazing how this works, in domestic and sexual violence—how men have been largely erased from so much of the conversation about a subject that is centrally about men."

> Violence against women is not a women's issue alone. It's a man's issue as well. . . . So to all of the guys out there—you have to step up. That's how we can change the culture on campus and around the country to one that understands no means no.
>
> —Joe Biden, former vice president, speaking at the University of Illinois at Urbana-Champaign, April 23, 2015

In 2016 Laura Niemi, assistant professor of social psychology and global justice at the University of Toronto in Canada, and Liane Young of the Morality Lab at Boston College in Chestnut Hill, Massachusetts, conducted a study. They presented two versions of a rape scenario to study participants. In both versions, the general outline of the scenario was the same: a man (Dan) flirts with a woman (Lisa) at a party, spikes her drink, and then assaults her. In one version, Niemi and Young described the scenario with the man as the subject: *Dan approached Lisa*, putting the focus on the person who committed the crime. For other participants, they put the victim as the subject: *Lisa was approached by Dan*. After hearing the story, the respondents were asked to describe what had happened in their own words. Niemi and Young rated the responses on a scale of victim blaming. Niemi and Young discovered that victim blaming was less likely among the people who had heard the story with Dan (the perpetrator) as the subject.

Changing the way we talk about sexual harassment and assault is part of dismantling rape culture. Here are some recommendations:

Use accurate language. Words matter. *Rape* is not *having sex* or *making love*. It is an act of sexual violence. Survivors don't *seduce* their assailants; they are *assaulted*. Women controlled by sex traffickers (people who sell other people, mostly girls and women, for sex) are not *sex workers*; they are *enslaved*. Using the active voice—"a man raped a woman"—reminds readers that a perpetrator committed an illegal act. The passive voice—"a woman was raped"—erases the rapist and creates the false illusion of a perpetrator-free crime.

Put the focus in the right place. Describing a victim's clothes, past sexual history, and behaviors (such as drinking) around the time of the assault blames the victim for the crime that occurred. The burden of responsibility for a sex crime should always fall on the perpetrator. Similarly, focusing on how difficult it is for the perpetrator to listen to victim impact statements or how negatively the perpetrator's life will be affected by jail time erases the fact that his experience will never be as traumatic as that of the victim, nor that the victim had no choice in the matter.

Avoid stereotypes. If the case involves a marginalized person (or people), avoid negative stereotypes, especially if they feed rape myths about the "perfect victim" and the "deviant rapist."

Tell the whole story. Sexual assault is not just a single isolated event with no larger meaning. The whole story is that experts view rape as a public health issue. Any community in which members are at risk of violent assault is not safe. The whole story is that rape is also a social justice issue. Advocates point out that any community in which victims from marginalized groups are treated unfairly is not a just society.

CHAPTER SEVEN
YES MEANS YES, NO MEANS NO

When Luke Howard's girlfriend of four months broke up with him, he couldn't accept it. Instead, he bought a piano and had it dropped off at a city park in the center of Bristol, England. His plan was to play music nonstop until his ex took him back. The media was all over the story. Most reporters described Howard's idea as a grand, romantic gesture. Headlines read, "Heartbreaking reason this lovelorn man has vowed to play the piano non-stop in public" and "Hopeless romantic isn't going to stop playing the piano until his true love takes him back." However, many women saw things differently. On Twitter @sianushka said, "Men, women are allowed to leave you. You are not entitled to a girlfriend. Media, stop romanticising controlling, stalker behaviour." Activist Ijeoma Oluo wrote, "I hope that parents will walk their young boys by this pathetic display to point and say, 'THIS is what happens when you feel entitled to women. You end up being a self-obsessed 34 year old embarrassing himself in the middle of [a f-ing] park. . . .' Women are not your property. You are not entitled to our company. We do not exist to make you better, or happier, or more complete. Our autonomous decisions are not a reflection on your manhood."

Howard called off the stunt, but not because he understood what women were telling him about his aggressive behavior toward a woman who had told him no. Instead, it was because a stranger punched him in the head at four in the morning. Howard wrote, "I do not blame or in fact feel anything negative towards anyone who has commented on what I decided to do. On the contrary, the lack of understanding just reminds me of how very rare a thing pure love actually is."

NO, NO, NO! YES?

The piano player thought he was fighting for love. He thought if he pushed and pushed, eventually his ex would return to him.

Where did that idea come from?

Pop culture is full of stories that glorify sexually aggressive male characters and blur the lines between sex and violence. Many movies contain scenes in which a man and a woman begin as enemies. They argue with each other, and eventually the tension turns to attraction and finally sex. The dominant message in pop culture is that eventually women will give in to men's sexual aggression. *No, no, no* will eventually turn into *yes*. According to journalist Anna North, "Boys learn at a young age, from pop culture, their elders, and their peers, that it's normal to have to convince a woman to have sex, and that repeated small violations of her boundaries are an acceptable way to do so—perhaps even the only way."

Pop culture also presents various sex crimes as sexy, funny, and entertaining. In the *Twilight* series of books and movies by Stephenie Meyer, vampire Edward Cullen spends too much time sneaking into the bedroom of the human girl Bella and watching her sleep. It's presented as romantic, when in fact, it's breaking and entering. Other shows,

In *Goldfinger*, a James Bond movie from 1964, Bond (played by Sean Connery) corners an enemy lesbian cat burglar named Pussy Galore (played by Honor Blackman) in a barn. He forces her down to kiss her as she tries to fight him off. The film then follows standard rape culture mythology. Pussy Galore eventually gives in to Bond, and the two become lovers.

mostly billed as comedies, hinge on horny men trying to get a look at naked women. There are plots that involve hidden cameras in bedrooms and peepholes in shower stalls. This is a crime called unlawful surveillance. And it doesn't stop there. An ad from the Bloomingdale's department store promoted illegally drugging women. The ad used the slogan "Spike your best friend's eggnog when they're not looking." Bud Light ran an ad that read, "The perfect beer for removing no from your vocabulary for the night." The lyrics of Robin Thicke's song "Blurred Lines" glorify sexual violence. Rape shows up as a frequent plot point on TV shows such as *Westworld* and *Game of Thrones*. It is also in movies such as *Mad Max: Fury Road* and *Red Sparrow*. Jeremy Slater, a movie producer who reads hundreds of movie scripts each year, says, "I was shocked by the number that had [rape]. I would say out of those 200 scripts, there were probably 30 or 40 of them that opened with a rape or had a pretty savage rape at some point."

Does constant exposure to media that glorifies sexual aggression turn boys into rapists? No, but it does set up conditions that allow sexually aggressive behavior to flourish. Sexually aggressive behaviors can, when taken to an extreme, lead to rape. When guys like Howard ignore *no* because they think this is how romantic relationships work, interpersonal relationships can get ugly fast. According to Julie Beck, a journalist at the *Atlantic*, "Our [US] culture is beginning to . . . question the value of romanticizing stories where one person chases another, or wears her down, or drags her along against her will. But recognizing the flaws in these ideas doesn't make them go away. They still float in the spaces between people; they are the sludge through which we have to swim as we try to see each other clearly."

What is the sludge in rape culture?

The belief that men don't have to listen when a woman says *no*.

The belief that men can objectify the bodies of women.

The belief that women who like sex are sluts.

The belief that men can't be expected to control their sexual urges.

The belief that women are responsible for keeping horny men at bay.

The belief that women don't have a right to decide what they do with their bodies.

The belief that rape isn't really a big deal.

TOLD TO SAY NO

From slut shaming to sexual objectification, the way people talk about the female body is central to rape culture. Negative and often contradictory beliefs about women's bodies and women's sexuality contribute to the high rate of assault. One in five American women will be sexually assaulted in their lifetime. Yet the sex education curriculum for teens in US schools often reinforces elements of rape culture. In fact, teens are receiving less sex education overall. Newer laws since the 1980s restrict what teachers can present to teens.

In the 1970s, high school students across the United States knew a lot about sex and reproduction. In school they took comprehensive sex education classes. Students were taught the details of human reproduction, menstruation, sex, pregnancy, and pregnancy prevention. Students were taught that sometimes two people might have sex for no other reason than physical pleasure.

The sex education curriculum changed radically when religious conservatives gained political power in the 1980s. During this time, HIV/AIDS had emerged, hitting the gay community first. Fear of the unknown disease and homophobia drove conservative lawmakers to shift the focus of sex ed to abstinence. The goal of abstinence-only lessons is to promote virginity. It does not talk about shaping healthy, safe relationships or understanding safer sex practices. Depending on the school district, much of the curriculum—if the school even offers sex ed classes—shames sexually active teens and condemns LGBTQ+ sexuality. Some lessons reinforce negative gender stereotypes. Some include information that is factually incorrect. These programs contribute to rape culture by promoting falsehoods about sex, sexuality,

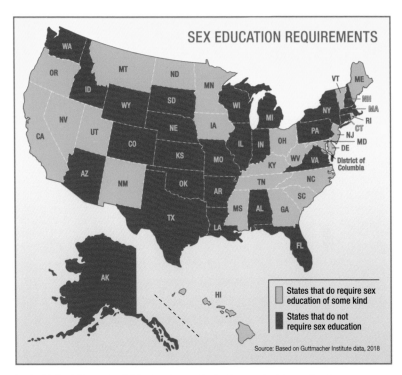

SEX EDUCATION REQUIREMENTS

States that do require sex education of some kind

States that do not require sex education

Source: Based on Guttmacher Institute data, 2018

In the United States, individual states make their own decisions about sex education in the public schools. Fewer than half require sex education of any kind. In states that do have sex education classes, information is often limited to abstinence and prevention of HIV/AIDS.

and gender roles. And they don't protect against teen pregnancy either. A 2017 study by Laura Lindberg from the Guttmacher Institute confirmed earlier public health research that showed that abstinence-only programs do not delay intercourse, reduce rates of sexually transmitted diseases, or reduce the rate of teen pregnancy. Lindberg emphasizes that abstinence-only sex education programs are unethical. They harm young people because they withhold critical information.

PAID TO SAY YES

Without comprehensive sex education, young people turned to the internet. As of 2018, teens are getting most of their sex education from online pornography. According to Bryant Paul, a professor in the Media School at Indiana University in Bloomington, boys first see porn when they are around thirteen. Girls' first exposure occurs around the age of fourteen. As one teenage boy said, "There's nowhere else to learn about sex." A 2015 study by Emily Rothman at Boston University's School of Public Health confirmed this. The majority of the teens she surveyed reported using porn as their main source of information about sex.

But just what are teens learning? Not a whole lot about reality.

The bodies of many porn actors are surgically altered to fit an extreme version of sexiness. Sexual stamina in porn is often unrealistic. So are the sexual behaviors. Porn often highlights male aggression and violence. In a 2010 study, 88 percent of scenes in porn videos showed male verbal or physical aggression toward women. Women are usually shown enjoying these behaviors. Consent is a nonexistent part of the story. That's because writers and directors script the sex acts in advance—without adding consent to the story line. Porn performers consent to participate in the sex acts before filming starts, and they are paid according to what they agree to do.

Pornography is highly staged and choreographed. Yet a 2016 survey of 1,001 kids in Great Britain between the ages of eleven and sixteen showed that 53 percent of boys and 39 percent of girls who had seen pornography thought that it showed realistic sex. Sex educator Al Vernacchio at the Friends' Central School in Wynnewood, Pennsylvania, points out that porn "shows misogynistic, unhealthy representations of relationships. You can't learn relationship skills from porn, and if you are looking for pleasure and connection, porn can't teach you how to have those."

Evidence from extensive interviews with young people suggests that teen sexual behavior is influenced by pornography. For example, one teen boy said about rough sex in porn, "It gets in your head. If this girl [in porn] wants it, then maybe the majority of girls want it." When asked about getting consent for anal sex, another boy said, "I would just do it [anal penetration]." He added that since the women in porn like it, all women must like it. As for girls, many think that they should enjoy and want the things that happen to women in porn, so they agree to these behaviors with their partners. One girl said that she and her friends think certain porn behaviors are gross but that "you gotta do what you gotta do."

YES MEANS YES

In 2008 former Tennessee state senator Doug Henry said to his colleagues, "Rape, ladies and gentlemen, is not today what rape was. Rape, when I was learning these things, was the violation of a chaste woman [virgin], against her will, by some party not her spouse. Today it's simply, 'Let's don't go forward with this act.'" If you're saying, "Yes, exactly!" then you support the idea that enthusiastic consent should be part of every sexual interaction. And that exchange would look something like this:

> *Do you want to have sex with me?*
> *Yes, I really do want to have sex with you.*

Age of Consent

Age-of-consent laws are meant to protect young people from sexual predators. These laws say that minors aren't mature enough to give consent to sex. When an adult has sex with a minor, laws view it as statutory rape, even if the minor claimes to be a willing participant. Adult sexual predators often spend weeks or months using compliments and favors to manipulate their potential victims into agreeing to sexual behaviors they don't really want to do (a process called grooming).

Age-of-consent laws also sometimes apply to teenage sexual behavior. In some states, an eighteen-year-old having consensual sex with a seventeen-year-old would be considered statutory rape. Some states have close-in-age exemptions (also known as Romeo and Juliet laws). This means that if two consenting teens who are very close in age choose to have sex, they would not be prosecuted for sex crimes. However, not all states have this exception. You can look up "age of consent" and "close-in-age exemptions" for every US state and many countries at the website www.ageofconsent.net.

How are teens supposed to learn how to have conversations about sexual consent? Porn doesn't model consent. Pop culture media rarely shows partners actively seeking and giving consent. Abstinence-only sex education focuses on *no*, not *yes*. And most parents are so uncomfortable with the idea that their teens might be sexually active that they don't offer guidance for how to navigate consent.

California and other states are trying to do something about this. For example, in 2014 California enacted the Yes Means Yes law. The text of the bill defines consent as the "affirmative, conscious, and voluntary agreement to engage in sexual activity. . . . Lack of protest or resistance does not mean consent, nor does silence mean consent. Affirmative consent must be ongoing throughout a sexual activity and can be revoked [taken back] at any time. The existence of a dating relationship between the persons involved, or the fact of past sexual relations between them, should never by itself be assumed to be an indicator of consent."

An extremely drunk person can't give consent.

An unconscious person can't give consent.

A sleeping person can't give consent.

Another key part of the California law is that a person can change their mind in the middle of sex. They can decide they don't want to proceed—and their partner has to respect that choice and stop. As Kate Harding points out, "[Consent] is not a black-and-white contract you sign before having sex, but an ongoing series of communications between sexual partners, whether that takes place during a single encounter or over several years. . . . When you become sexually active, you quickly learn that sex as it's practiced in the real world nearly always demands small, quick renegotiations as you go along." It's all about talking to each other throughout the sexual encounter.

Asking for consent is just the beginning. Maya Dusenbery, editorial director at the blog *Feministing*, says, "I don't want us to ever lose sight of the fact that consent is not the goal. Seriously, God help us if the best we can say about the sex we have is that it was consensual." To get from consent—"yes, I want to have sex with you"—to a mutually satisfying intimate encounter requires intention. And good experiences don't just happen. One of the most important things people can do to dismantle rape culture is to encourage and talk about healthy sexuality and healthy relationships. That may or may not include sex.

Dismantling rape culture also means helping each person in a sexual encounter feel satisfied. That means sharing power and making decisions together. It means speaking up for what you want and don't want—and not faking it. Some feminists talk about *bad sexist sex* as part of rape culture. It means that only one of the people in a sexual encounter—usually a man— is calling the shots. And even if the sex is consensual, it's not great sex when only one person is having all the fun.

Having mutually pleasurable relationships requires changing the way we think about sex. Sex educator Al Vernacchio says, "I've always disliked comparing sex to baseball, in part due to the gender assumptions it makes. . . . We're not playing on the same team; we're playing against each other—so someone wins and someone loses. Another way to look at the gender roles in this model is to see boys as the players and the girls as the field upon which the game is played."

The baseball model of sex is part of rape culture because it presents male sexual aggression as the norm. Vernacchio suggests that we think about sex not as a game with winners and losers but like sharing a pizza with someone. Sometimes you're really hungry for pizza. You want it. That's cool. Sometimes you aren't in the mood for pizza, and that's okay too. But whether or not you eat pizza is up to you. It's a choice. When two people want to share a pizza (or have sex), then they need to talk about what each of them needs to feel satisfied. There are lots of different ways to make a pizza. If you talk about your options, share your desires, and come up with ideas that make you and your partner happy and safe, then you are more likely to have a healthy and satisfying experience.

You're also dismantling rape culture.

CHAPTER EIGHT
SPEAKING OUT, STANDING UP

Comedian Daniel Tosh is a clean-cut white guy with perfect teeth. He's also known for pushing the boundary between comedy and offensiveness. He's the guy who tweets with the hashtag #deadbabies, after all. In 2012 he was doing a stand-up set at the Laugh Factory in Hollywood and asked for prompts from the audience. Someone in the audience suggested rape. Tosh relished the challenge and said something about rape jokes always being funny. A woman in the audience stood up and said, "Actually rape jokes are never funny." He heckled back, coming up with what he thought were hilarious rape scenarios. For the woman in the audience, his comments came across as threatening and a little dangerous. Author and rape survivor Roxane Gay says, "Rape humor is designed to remind women that they are still not quite equal. . . . When that woman stood up and said, 'No, rape is not funny,' she did not consent to participating in a culture that encourages [dismissive] attitudes toward sexual violence and the concerns of women."

Shortly after the comedy club incident, author Lindy West challenged Tosh and other comedians about the jokes they make at the expense of rape victims. She pointed out that at least one in four female college students has been sexually assaulted. "If you're a comic performing to a reasonably full room, there's a pretty good chance that at least one person in the audience has been sexually assaulted. . . . When you make a joke in that room that trivializes rape or mocks rape victims, you are deliberately harming those people," West said. Trolls on the internet responded by sending her hundreds of graphic rape threats.

West gets that comedy is a perfect place to push boundaries. All the same, she points out that the best comedy punches up. That means that the butt of an excellent joke should be the person with power in the situation. Making a joke at the expense of a rape victim is just mean. Comedian John Mulaney has a joke about rape that perfectly illustrates punching up. "Late at night, on the street, women will

Lindy West writes opinion pieces for the *New York Times*. She also writes for *This American Life*, the *Guardian*, *Cosmopolitan*, *Jezebel*, and other news sources. She founded *I Believe You, It's Not Your Fault*, an advice blog for teens who want help dealing with rape culture. She is also the cofounder of the reproductive rights campaign #ShoutYourAbortion. Her first book, *Shrill: Notes from a Loud Woman*, is a memoir. It was published in 2016.

see me as a threat. That is funny—yeah! That *is* funny. It's kind of flattering in its own way, but at the same time it's weird because, like, I'm still afraid of being kidnapped."

This joke is smart because it shows that Mulaney, a young white guy, knows that women out at night are usually scared of men. The joke is funny because it points out his vulnerability—that he's scared at night too. Comedy like this deflates or reverses the expected power structure and is one way to dismantle rape culture.

ELIMINATING SEXUAL VIOLENCE

After more than a century of work by feminists, LGBTQ+ activists, and civil rights activists and allies (people who support others in the efforts to eliminate oppression), #MeToo and #TimesUp catapulted sexual harassment and assault into a fervent national—and international—conversation. Survivors of abuse and assault and their allies are speaking out and demanding change. They are finally being heard.

On May 25, 2018, Harvey Weinstein was charged with two counts of rape and sexual assault. New charges came forward in July 2018 alleging that Weinstein had assaulted a third woman and had a pattern of sex crimes. He pleaded not guilty to all charges and was released on bail. If convicted, Weinstein faces a minimum of ten years in prison with the possibility of twenty-five years to life.

Weinstein is not the only person to be called out. Men in power are resigning or being fired or being put on indefinite leave from their jobs for sexually unacceptable behaviors. They are being charged with sex crimes and brought before juries. Tolerance for business as usual is over. People are finally coming to grips with the pervasiveness of sexual harassment and assault in families, in schools, at work, and in the streets. All of this is positive change, but there is still much work to be done.

First, eliminating sexual violence requires that people take an intersectional approach. Chris Linder from the University of Georgia in Athens and Jessica Harris from the University of California in Los Angeles point out, "The root cause of sexual violence is oppression, in all of its manifestations, including racism, cis-sexism, heterosexism, ableism and sexism. Oppression results from people abusing power or lacking consciousness about how power influences their own and others' experiences." People with privilege can be good allies for people with less power if they take the time to educate themselves about the oppression faced by others.

For example, men must begin to more fully understand that women experience a near-constant threat of assault. White people must acknowledge that the justice system and other institutions of power often treat people of color unfairly. Abled people must be aware of the extra vulnerabilities of disabled people. Heterosexual and cisgender peoples must be aware of LGBTQ+ issues. Most people are privileged in some ways and oppressed in others. To work for social justice of any kind, we must be willing to listen and learn. Author Swati Avasthi says, "When I first started decolonizing [striving to understand privilege and oppression] and getting woke [becoming aware of privilege and oppression], a friend said to me, 'It's all about who you listen to.' So I learned this: listen and defer to those who have more experience than you. . . . Just start believing them when they speak."

Second, eliminating sexual violence requires laws, institutional policies, and educational programs that address sexual harassment and assault in all elements of life—at home, in schools, at work, and in public spaces. Legislative solutions include enforcing existing laws such as Title IX, as well as passing new laws such as requiring police departments to test every single rape kit. Policy solutions include insisting that schools and workplaces enforce zero tolerance of sexual harassment and make it safe and easy for victims to report abusers. Educational solutions include workplace sensitivity training and public service campaigns. One educational campaign created by the police department in Vancouver, British Columbia, stated, "Just because she isn't saying no, doesn't mean she's saying yes. Sex without consent equals sexual assault. Don't be *that* guy."

> "We are . . . daughters, wives, mothers, sisters and human beings. We come in peace, but we mean business. . . . Just as we have the power to shape culture, we also have the power to undo a culture that does not serve us well."
>
> —Janelle Monáe, actor and musician, Grammy Awards, 2018

Third, eliminating sexual violence requires more than simply punishing offenders. It requires healing in the broadest sense—for survivors, perpetrators, and families. Restorative justice is one framework for this healing. By design, the US legal system pits an accuser against a defendant. The jury weighs evidence and decides whom to believe. Restorative justice focuses on healing the violation of relationships and the damage done to communities. Alissa Ackerman is an associate professor of criminal justice at the

University of Washington Tacoma, and Jill Levenson is a licensed clinical social worker. They say, "A key component of restorative justice frameworks is that offenders must accept responsibility for their actions. Equally important is the survivor's narrative, as much of the healing process stems from telling one's story and being heard. The process allows victims to be heard, to seek the acknowledgement of culpability [guilt] they need, and for perpetrators to hear, firsthand, the personal narrative of suffering they have caused that permeates [spreads], like a ripple effect, across time and relationships." The restorative justice process can occur in facilitated meetings, in support groups, or in community settings. It may include teachers, peers, family members, or religious leaders in addition to the victims and perpetrators. It is not a replacement for the criminal justice system. Instead, it can complement the legal system or substitute for it, especially in communities of color who cannot turn to the police. Rape survivor Claire Chung met with her rapist in two restorative justice sessions. She said the conversations helped her. "Hearing the offender say sorry has been a hugely positive step in my recovery and it has helped me overcome the perception that I am just another forgotten statistic."

Fourth, eliminating sexual violence requires each of us to take steps to dismantle rape culture in our everyday lives. Every single one of us can be part of the solution starting right now. To dismantle rape culture, we must pay attention to the aspects of rape culture throughout our daily lives. We must call them out and refuse to participate in them. These questions are helpful starting points:

- Where do you see gender stereotypes? Do you see men expressing toxic masculinity? Where and how?
- Do others make excuses for male sexual aggression with phrases such as *boys will be boys* or *locker room talk*? When and where do people encourage it?

- Are women objectified in your favorite videos, TV shows, and movies? How? Do women objectify themselves in social media and pop culture?
- Where do you observe slut shaming? Does the dress code at your school target female students unfairly?
- How prevalent is sexual harassment at your school or workplace? Is it ignored or addressed?
- How is sexual assault portrayed on TV and in movies? Does *no* turn into *yes* during sexual interactions? Would the actions of male characters be considered illegal in real life?
- How are sex crimes covered in the local news? Do headlines and commentaries blame the victim? When survivors come forward, do people believe them?
- Do you, your friends, and your family talk openly and comfortably about sex and consent?

FOR THE GUYS: A CALL TO ACTION

Historically, sexual assault and domestic violence have been lumped with childcare and reproductive health care as women's issues. Jackson Katz disagrees. In his TED Talk from 2012, Katz says, "I don't see these as women's issues that some good men help out with. In fact, I'm going to argue that these are men's issues, first and foremost." Through the organization Mentors in Violence Prevention, which he cofounded, Katz works with the military, with athletic teams, and in other male-dominated environments to teach men how to work toward the elimination of sexual and domestic violence. He points out that men benefit from the power structures of patriarchy, so they are in a position to use their privilege to benefit women and girls. Men who want to be good allies can use their power to help dismantle rape culture.

Studies show that teachers tend to pay more attention to boys than to girls. They may call on them more often and generally talk to them more. They tolerate behaviors in boys that they don't tolerate in girls. Teachers also tend to offer both more praise and more criticism to boys than to girls. Students can help one another by making sure girls get a fair chance to speak in class.

It starts with listening to the people, mostly women, who take the brunt force of rape culture head on. Resist the impulse to dispute or dismiss their stories of harassment and misogyny. Take their experiences seriously. If the stories make you uncomfortable or defensive, that's normal. Listen, listen, and listen some more. Listening is a huge part of learning and reshaping attitudes.

> "We need more men with the guts, with the courage, with the strength, with the moral integrity to break our complicit silence and challenge each other and stand with women and not against them."
>
> —Jackson Katz, cofounder of Mentors in Violence Prevention, TED Talk, 2012

And just as important, look for opportunities to actively counter elements of rape culture. For example, if a girl in class is trying to make a point but keeps getting talked over by male students, make space for her. Say something like, "I really want to hear what you have to say."

Don't let misogynistic or other hate-based comments or rape jokes slide. You can call out the comments and jokes by saying, "I don't think that's funny" or "I don't like jokes that put down other people." If they insist the comments and jokes are funny, say, "I wouldn't want anyone talking that way about my sister or my mom."

> "Inherently, having privilege isn't bad, but it's how you use it, and you have to use it in service of other people."
>
> —Tarana Burke, founder of the #MeToo movement, *Guardian*, 2018

Consider how you can make others feel physically safe. In most public situations, women are on high alert to the potential for danger. Keep that in mind and give women extra space, especially at night or in secluded places. If you think you or your group of friends might make someone you are approaching nervous, cross to the other side of the street. Slow down so you aren't walking right on someone's heels. You know that you're not a danger, but they don't.

Most of all, take time for self-reflection. How has rape culture affected you? Are there gentler parts of your personality that you've suppressed because they are considered too feminine? To fit into American society, have you tried to copy harmful stereotypes about masculinity? Look for a supportive men's group in your area—or start one. Talk with other young men about how to change your own attitudes and behaviors. Think of safe ways to express feelings and vulnerability. Learn from positive role models about how to be a good man and a good ally.

BYSTANDER ACTION

Jackson Katz and others who work to eliminate sexual violence know that bystander action is essential to dismantling rape culture. Sexual harassment and assault are power plays—one person exerting power over another, more vulnerable person. And because bystanders aren't the target, they have a different kind of power, one that can be used to keep someone else safe. Some anti-violence programs teach three steps for taking action: direct, distract, delegate.

Direct means "doing something immediately." It could be responding to a rape joke with "Hey, that's not cool," or if someone's hitting on your friend and she's not into it, saying "You need to back off because she's not interested." Taking direct action might mean seeing a barely conscious person being tugged into a back room and intervening by alerting someone and getting help for that person.

Distract means "finding a way to derail sexist comments and unwelcome sexual attentions." For example, if a man is hitting on a woman at a bus stop and she is visibly uncomfortable, find a nonthreatening way to interrupt the interaction. Try asking her for directions or pretending to be a friend and starting a conversation.

Delegate means "getting help." If you're worried about a situation between two people that seems threatening and taking direct action seems unsafe, engage others. Ask people nearby for assistance. Call the police or 911. Don't be the person who takes a cell phone video while someone is assaulted. Don't be the person who walks away without trying to help.

CAN WE FLIRT?
RELATIONSHIPS WITHOUT RAPE CULTURE

In the wake of #MeToo, some people have protested that they are confused about how to move forward in romantic and sexual relationships. Some have asked about flirting. Is it still okay? Well, yes. Being a decent, respectful person is not that hard. You can flirt without

Flirting is okay, and it's fun—as long as the person with whom you are flirting responds positively, with smiles and accepting behavior. If they don't, back off.

being a jerk. The key is to pay attention to the other person's cues. Do they seem interested in you in the first place? Do they smile at you when they see you or when you say hello? If not, then don't flirt with that person. If yes, start slowly, with simple compliments. *I like seeing you* or *You look so nice today*. If the person stiffens or the lines of their face go hard or they get angry, they're uncomfortable with what you said. Back off. If they laugh or smile or say something flirtatious back, then you know things are okay.

In December 2017, comedian Kate Willett used her Facebook page to lay out the difference between flirting and harassment.

> I love to be flirted with. I don't like being sexually harassed.
> These two things are not the same, and if you're arguing the
> point "now men can't flirt anymore," you don't understand
> what flirting is or you're just pretending not to in order to
> set up [an] argument in favor of sexual harassment. Good

flirting is fundamentally empathetic. It's about building desire and it's often pretty subtle. It's paying such deep attention to another person's emotions and body language that you create more intimacy with them. It's a two-way, playful, fun exchange that makes everyone feel good. Sexual harassment is the opposite. It's [without] empathy and it's about forcing your will upon another person without having any regard for their desire. You're comparing a paint brush to a wrecking ball.

To dismantle rape culture, all people need to reject rigid gender roles. This plays out in interpersonal relationships. One of the toxic myths of rape culture is that men don't care about emotional connection. In fact, as former football player Terry Crews says, "Even though we're trained not to admit it, men want intimacy—for someone to see us for who we are and love us regardless. But to get true intimacy, you have to be emotionally open." A healthy relationship of any kind means shared satisfaction. Both people need to feel good about what's happening. Don't assume you know what your partner likes or wants. Ask. Talk about your feelings and emotions too. Being close to someone isn't just about holding hands or having sex. It's about understanding each other's feelings and values and dreams.

Perhaps the biggest myth of rape culture is that the constellation of beliefs and behaviors is natural and can't be changed. That's just not true. In the last two hundred years, human culture has seen profound global changes toward greater equality and justice. Dismantling rape culture will be another huge step forward, and you can be part of the effort.

Envisioning a World without Rape Culture

"I almost can't conceive of a world where I go for a walk by myself without half an ear turned over my shoulder and my phone or keys clutched in my hand. What would it be like to be able to stride through the forested paths in the moonlight and just feel the night air on my skin—not that constant tightness in my chest and adrenaline pushing my steps?" —Holly Westlund

"It would be nice to not worry about my daughter walking home at night or any time really." —Jim Burkhart

"Ending rape culture would mean a sense of freedom to move freely throughout our lives in ways that many of us don't even imagine right now." —Kristi Wallace Knight

"**That girls would be free to dress as crazy as they want** in skimpy outfits without fear of attack. That when it's hot we can go topless without any sexualization like men can, that gendered terminology is so unnecessary that it no longer exists." —Mira Reisberg

"That girls be encouraged, starting with their parents and teachers, to speak up and be themselves without being told they are too abrupt or opinionated. **Abolish the idea that strong, smart women are a threat or somehow not the feminine norm.**" —Wendy Myers

"Another thing that is always present . . . is trying to speak out in a group setting knowing that many of the males there are eager to cut you off, interrupt you, 'clarify' and/or 'correct' your idea/s, and undermine anything you have to say. . . . It would be nice to be able to open your mouth in a group setting without having that tension of wondering if you'll be 'allowed' to finish your thought." —Cindy Collins Taylor

"Women wouldn't be harassed in [scientific professions]. There would be no 'she's there [because] of the way she looks' and no 'if you need a raise, go be a stripper.' **Women would feel safe doing fieldwork wherever their science took them**, instead of worrying about who they might encounter and what could potentially happen." —Anne Estes Hearn

"I try to imagine what a world would look like where women had equal professional opportunities and access, and how much farther ahead we could be in sustainability and compassionate entrepreneurship." —Kiersi Burkhart

"More women in leadership positions throughout society, better healthcare and education, strong social responsibility for the environment and for each other, raising men to maturity with an openness to their emotional lives and a deep awareness of the emotional lives of other living things." —T. Edward Bak

"If a man said something inappropriate, every other man in the room would turn and look at him like he had a third eye, instead of giving him a high five."
—Andrew Stoehr

"When both men and women are free to say either 'no' or 'yes' to sex without fear of shame, violence, and retribution." —DeAnna Smith

"It would be a world in which I can travel alone without caution, a world in which sex is always a mutual, joyful, life affirming event, **a world where women's humanity isn't smothered by dominance and oppression**, and men are allowed the full span of theirs. Mostly, a world without rape culture would manifest in true, deep love, reverence and care for this gorgeous, wild, amazing planet of ours and all of her creatures." —Janice Garceau

Source Notes

5   Juliet Macur and Nate Schweber, "Rape Case Unfolds on Web and Splits City," *New York Times*, December 16, 2012, http://www.nytimes.com /2012/12/17/sports/high-school-football-rape-case-unfolds-online-and -divides-steubenville-ohio.html.

5   Jesus Diaz, "One Year Later: The Terrible Aftermath of the Steubenville Rape Case," *Jezebel*, September 9, 2016, https://jezebel.com/a-town -destroyed-for-what-two-people-did-dispatch-fr-1298509440/1326333146.

5   Diaz.

5   Ryan Broderick, "The Definitive Timeline of the Steubenville Rape Scandal," BuzzFeed, January 4, 2013, https://www.buzzfeed.com/ ryanhatesthis/the-definitive-timeline-of-the-steubenville-rape-s?utm _term=.jejPyOEmWA#.ypdoYj2PZB.

6   Eric Minor, Twitter post, March 16, 2013, 2:13 p.m., https://twitter.com /EricMinorWVU/status/313035214773420032.

6   Connor Simpson, "The Steubenville Victim Tells Her Story," *Atlantic*, March 16, 2013, https://www.theatlantic.com/national/archive/2013/03 /steubenville-victim-testimony/317302/.

8   Kate Harding, *Asking for It: The Rise of Rape Culture—and What We Can Do about It* (Boston: Da Capo Lifelong Books, 2015), 48.

8   Macur and Schweber, "Rape Case Unfolds."

8   David Lisak, "Understanding the Predatory Nature of Sexual Violence," *Sexual Assault Report* 14, no 4 (2011): 49.

10   *Merriam-Webster*, s.v., "sexual harassment," accessed November 2, 2017, https://www.merriam-webster.com/dictionary/sexual%20harassment."

10   "Sexual Assault," RAINN, accessed January 5, 2018, https://www.rainn.org /articles/sexual-assault.

11   Joanne Smith, Mandy Van Deven, and Meghan Huppuch, *Hey, Shorty! A Guide to Combating Sexual Harassment and Violence in Schools and on the Streets* (New York: Feminist, 2011), 38.

11–12   Betty Friedan, *The Feminine Mystique* (New York: W. W. Norton, 1963), accessed December 12, 2017, https://archive.org/stream/TheFeminineMystique /TheFeminineMystique-Betty-Friedan_djvu.txt.

12   Shannon Ridgway, "25 Everyday Examples of Rape Culture," Everyday Feminism, March 10, 2014, https://everydayfeminism.com/2014/03 /examples-of-rape-culture/.

12–13   Harding, *Asking for It*, 2.

14   Sameer Rao, "Tarana Burke, Ai-Jen Poo, Saru Jayaraman and Other Activists on Why They Appeared at the Golden Globes," Colorlines,

January 8, 2018, https://www.colorlines.com/articles/tarana-burke-ai-jen-poo-saru-jayaraman-and-other-activists-why-they-appeared-golden-globes.

17 Alyssa Milano, Twitter post, October 15, 2017, 1:21 p.m., https://twitter
    .com/Alyssa_Milano/status/919659438700670976/photo/1.

18 Cat Milspo, Twitter thread, October 15, 2017, 1:28 p.m., https://twitter
    .com/CatMilspo/status/919661373814136832.

18 Najwa Zebian, Twitter post, October 15, 2017, 5:07 p.m., https://twitter
    .com/najwazebian/status/919716293602893825?lang=en.

18 Kate Brown, Twitter post, October 18, 2017, 3:35 p.m., https://twitter.com
    /KateBrownForOR/status/920780284391514112.

18 TheBetht, Twitter post, October 18, 2017, 2:29 p.m., https://twitter.com
    /GrapheqDesign/status/920763776898600960.

18 Samara Wilde, Twitter post, October 18, 2017, 2:22 p.m., https://twitter
    .com/The_Wilde_Chick/status/920762125072699392.

18 Sarah L. Sheppard, Twitter post, October 18, 2017, 1:34 p.m., https://
    twitter.com/scrappysheppard/status/920750015919702016.

18 Julissa Arce, Twitter post, October 18, 2017, 11:17 p.m., https://twitter.com
    /julissaarce/status/920715516502671360.

18 Geisterwand, Twitter post, October 15, 2017, 10:31 p.m., https://twitter
    .com/Geisterwand/status/919797920303591424.

19 Susan Brownmiller, *Against Our Will: Men, Women and Rape* (New York:
    Ballantine Books, 1975), 256.

19 Jodi Kantor and Megan Twohey, "Harvey Weinstein Paid Off Sexual
    Harassment Accusers for Decades," *New York Times*, October 5, 2017,
    https://www.nytimes.com/2017/10/05/us/harvey-weinstein-harassment
    -allegations.html.

20 Cassandra Santiago and Doug Criss, "An Activist, a Little Girl, and the
    Heartbreaking Origin of 'Me Too,'" *CNN*, October 17, 2017, http://www
    .cnn.com/2017/10/17/us/me-too-tarana-burke-origin-trnd/index.html.

20 Santiago and Criss.

21 Elizabeth Cady Stanton, "The Declaration of Sentiments, 1848," Friends of
    Women's Rights National Park, accessed May 20, 2018, http://www
    .womensrightsfriends.org/pdfs/1848_declaration_of_sentiments.pdf.

21 Stanton.

22 Kimberlé Crenshaw, "Why Intersectionality Can't Wait," *Washington Post*,
    September 24, 2015, https://www.washingtonpost.com/news/in-theory
    /wp/2015/09/24/why-intersectionality-cant-wait/.

23 Lulu Garcia-Navarro, "When Black Women's Stories of Sexual Abuse Are

Excluded from the National Narrative," *NPR*, *Weekend Edition Sunday*,
December 3, 2017, https://www.npr.org/2017/12/03/568133048/women-of
-color-and-sexual-harassment.

23 bell hooks, *Feminism Is for Everybody* (London: Pluto, 2000), viii.

24 Brianna Chambers, "Teenage Male Athletes Wear 'Wild Feminist' Shirts to
    Combat 'Locker Room Banter,'" *Atlanta Journal-Constitution*, October 18,
    2016, https://www.ajc.com/news/national/teenage-male-athletes-wear-wild
    -feminist-shirts-combat-locker-room-banter/snncXuJhGUzI12AbFicUbJ/.

25 Terry Crews, Twitter Moments, October 10, 2017, https://twitter.com/i
    /moments/917849599213158400.

26 "Terry Crews: Speaks Out on Being Victim of Sexual Harassment,"
    YouTube video, 07:44, posted by CelebNews18, November 2017, https://
    www.youtube.com/watch?v=2jNFymV3J-M.

26 "Time's Up Now," Time's Up, accessed January 12, 2018, https://www
    .timesupnow.com/.

26–27 "Time's Up Now."

27 Sophie Gilbert and Tori Latham, "Full Transcript: Oprah Winfrey's Speech
    at the Golden Globes," *Atlantic*, January 8, 2018, https://www.theatlantic
    .com/entertainment/archive/2018/01/full-transcript-oprah-winfreys-speech
    -at-the-golden-globes/549905/.

32 Lise Eliot, "Girl Brain, Boy Brain?," *Scientific American*, September 8, 2009,
    https://www.scientificamerican.com/article/girl-brain-boy-brain/.

33 Colleen Clemens, "What We Mean When We Say, 'Toxic Masculinity,'"
    Teaching Tolerance, December 11, 2017, https://www.tolerance.org/magazine
    /what-we-mean-when-we-say-toxic-masculinity.

33 "Transcript: Donald Trump's Taped Comments about Women," *New York
    Times*, October 8, 2016, https://www.nytimes.com/2016/10/08/us/donald
    -trump-tape-transcript.html.

34 Jason Katz, *The Macho Paradox: Why Some Men Hurt Women and How All
    Men Can Help* (Naperville, IL; Sourcebooks, 2006), 86.

34 Rachel Simmons, "When Middle Schoolers Say #MeToo," Huffington Post,
    December 15, 2017, https://www.huffingtonpost.com/entry/sexual
    -harassment-in-schools_us_5a32b145e4b00dbbcb5bb530?ncid=engmodush
    pmg00000003.

35 Harris O'Malley, "The Difference between Toxic Masculinity and Being a
    Man," Good Men Project, June 27, 2016, https://goodmenproject.com
    /featured-content/the-difference-between-toxic-masculinity-and-being-a
    -man-dg/.

35 Ryan Douglass, "More Men Should Learn the Difference between
    Masculinity and Toxic Masculinity," Huffington Post, August 4, 2017,

https://www.huffingtonpost.com/entry/the-difference-between-masculinity
-and-toxic-masculinity_us_59842e3ce4b0f2c7d93f54ce.

36 Colleen Clemens, "Toxic Masculinity Is Bad for Everyone: Why Teachers
    Must Disrupt Gender Norms Every Day," *Teaching Tolerance*, January 4,
    2018, https://www.tolerance.org/magazine/toxic-masculinity-is-bad-for
    -everyone-why-teachers-must-disrupt-gender-norms-every-day.

36 Jill Filipovic, "Offensive Feminism: The Conservative Gender Norms That
    Perpetuate Rape Culture, and How Feminists Can Fight Back," in *Yes
    Means Yes: Visions of Female Sexual Power and a World without Rape*, ed.
    Jaclyn Friedman and Jessica Valenti (Berkeley, CA: Seal, 2008), 19.

36 Alok Vaid-Menon, Twitter post, April 17, 2016, 11:55 a.m., https://twitter
    .com/alokvmenon/status/721773992223358977.

37 "Teenage Brothers on Sex, Social Media, and What Their Parents Don't
    Understand," *Cut*, March 5, 2018, https://www.thecut.com/2018/03/teen
    -brothers-on-sex-tech-and-what-their-parents-dont-get.html.

38 Hannah Pikaart, "Meet the Brooklyn Artist Who Lent Art-World Cred to
    Netflix 'She's Gotta Have It' Reboot," Artnet, December 11, 2017, https://
    news.artnet.com/art-world/brooklyn-artist-shes-gotta-have-it-1163225.

39 Katie Cappiello and Meg McInerney, eds. *Slut: A Play and Guidebook for
    Combating Sexism and Sexual Violence* (New York: Feminist, 2015), 54–55.

39–40 Cappiello and McInerney, 35–36.

40 "Title IX," Education Amendments of 1972 to the Civil Rights Act of 1964,
    Department of Labor, accessed September 19, 2018, https://www.dol.gov
    /oasam/regs/statutes/titleIX.htm.

41 Smith, Van Deven, and Huppuch, *Hey, Shorty!*, 62.

43 Barbara Kingsolver, "#MeToo Isn't Enough. Now Women Need to Get
    Ugly," *Guardian* (US ed.), January 16, 2018, https://www.theguardian.com
    /commentisfree/2018/jan/16/metoo-women-daughters-harassment-powerful
    -men.

46 Cappiello and McInerney, *Slut*, 26–27.

47 Caroline Heldman, "Sexual Objectification, Part 1: What Is It?," *Ms.
    Magazine* (blog), July 3, 2012, http://msmagazine.com/blog/2012/07/03
    /sexual-objectification-part-1-what-is-it/.

47 Javacia Harris, "A Woman's Worth," in *Yes Means Yes: Visions of Female
    Sexual Power and a World without Rape*, ed. Jaclyn Friedman and Jessica
    Valenti (Berkeley, CA: Seal, 2008), 62.

49 Cappiello and McInerney, *Slut*, 49–50.

49–50 Madeline Bruce, "School Dress Codes: A World of Double Standards,"
    Affinity, June 10, 2017, http://affinitymagazine.us/2017/06/10/school-dress
    -codes-a-world-of-double-standards/.

51 Emily McCombs, "Sexist School Dress Codes Are a Problem, and Oregon May Have the Answer," Huffington Post, September 5, 2017, https://www.huffingtonpost.com/entry/sexist-school-dress-codes-and-the-oregon-now-model_us_59a6cd7ee4b00795c2a318e5.

52 Jill Filipovic, "Offensive Feminism," 20.

53 Elliot Rodger, quoted in Harding, *Asking for It*, 191.

53 Quoted in Rebecca Solnit, "#YesAllWomen," *Men Explain Things to Me* (Chicago: Haymarket Books, 2014), 132–133.

54 Alan White, "Twitter Responds to Santa Barbara Shootings with #YesAllWomen Hashtag," Buzzfeed, May 25, 2014, https://www.buzzfeednews.com/article/alanwhite/twitter-responds-to-santa-barbara-shootings-with-yesallwomen.

55 Cappiello and McInerney, *Slut*, 47.

55 JR Thorpe, "Eight Things to Say to Shut Down Slut-Shamers (AKA, Haters)," Bustle, September 14, 2015, accessed May 24, 2018, https://www.bustle.com/articles/109881-8-things-to-say-to-shut-down-slut-shamers-aka-haters.

56 Thorpe.

56 Olga Khazan, "There's No Such Thing as a Slut," *Atlantic*, May 28, 2014, https://www.theatlantic.com/health/archive/2014/05/theres-no-such-thing-as-a-slut/371773/.

57 Michael McLaughlin, "What Kim Kardashian Taught Us about the Objectification of Women," Huffington Post, July 1, 2015, https://www.huffingtonpost.com/2015/07/01/kim-kardashian-objectification-women_n_7702852.html.

57 Lilith Hardie Lupica, "Kim Kardashian Pens an Essay in Response to Selfie Scandal," *Vogue*, March 10, 2016, https://www.vogue.com.au/celebrity/news/kim-kardashian-pens-an-essay-in-response-to-the-selfie-scandal/news-story/.

57 Ronnie Ritchie, "How Can You Tell If You're Being Empowered or Objectified? Ask This Simple Question," Everyday Feminism, April 13, 2015, https://everydayfeminism.com/2015/04/empowered-vs-objectified/.

57 Andy Khouri, Twitter post, January 14, 2018, 12:41 p.m., https://twitter.com/andykhouri/status/952641728120369152.

59 Ritchie, "How Can You Tell?"

59 Melissa Fabello, "Why We Need to Stop Conflating Objectification with Sexual Empowerment," Everyday Feminism, January 23, 2013, https://everydayfeminism.com/2013/01/conflating-sexual-objectification-with-sexual-empowerment/.

61 Anonymous, "I Went to the Hospital for a Rape Kit and It Was a 7-Hour Ordeal That Left Me Feeling Completely Alone," xoJane, November 13, 2015, https://www.xojane.com/issues/what-happens-during-a-rape-kit.

62 Soraya Chemaly, "How Police Still Fail Rape Victims," *Rolling Stone*, August 16, 2016, https://www.rollingstone.com/culture/features/how -police-still-fail-rape-victims-w434669

62–63 Chemaly.

63 Harding, *Asking for It*, 86.

63 Harding, 87.

64 Carla Correa and Meghan Louttit, "More Than 160 Women Say Larry Nassar Sexually Abused Them. Here Are His Accusers in Their Own Words," *New York Times*, January 24, 2018, https://www.nytimes.com /interactive/2018/01/24/sports/larry-nassar-victims.html.

64–65 Kristen Chatman, "I Am a Mom Who Was in the Exam Room While Dr. Larry Nassar Treated My Daughter," *Indianapolis Star*, February 8, 2018, https://www.indystar.com/story/opinion/readers/2018/02/08/larry-nassar -victim-mom-abuse-testimony-letter/319425002/.

66 Correa and Louttit, "More Than 160 Women."

66 Correa and Louttit.

67 Rebecca Epstein, Jamilia Blake, and Thalia González, "Girlhood Interrupted: The Erasure of Black Girls' Childhood," Social Science Research Network, June 27, 2017, http://dx.doi.org/10.2139/ssrn.3000695.

67 Kimberly Springer, "Queering Black Female Heterosexuality," in *Yes Means Yes: Visions of Female Sexual Power and a World without Rape*, ed. Jaclyn Friedman and Jessica Valenti (Berkeley, CA: Seal, 2008), 78.

68 Harding, *Asking for It*, 24.

68–69 Katie Baker, "Here Is the Powerful Letter the Stanford Victim Read Aloud to Her Attacker," BuzzFeed, June 3, 2016, https://www.buzzfeed.com /katiejmbaker/heres-the-powerful-letter-the-stanford-victim-read-to-her-ra.

71 Gabriella Paiella, "Brock Turner's Childhood Friend Blames His Felony Sexual Assault Conviction on Political Correctness," *Cut*, June 6, 2016, https://www.thecut.com/2016/06/brock-turners-friend-pens-letter-of -support.html.

72 Gabriella Paiella, "Here Is Brock Turner's Statement to the Judge," *Cut*, June 8, 2016, https://www.thecut.com/2016/06/here-is-brock-turners -statement-to-the-judge.html.

72 Michele Dauber, Twitter post, June 4, 2016, 9:58 p.m., https://twitter.com/ mldauber/status/739320585222660096.

72 Baker, "Here Is the Powerful Letter."

72–73 Harding, *Asking for It*, 25.

73 Smith, Van Deven, and Huppuch, *Hey, Shorty!*, 20.

74 Christine Rox, "I Am @Steenfox and I Wrote the Original Tweet 'What Were You Wearing?,'" xoJane, March 18, 2014, https://www.xojane.com /issues/i-am-steenfox-and-i-wrote-the-tweet-what-were-you-wearing.

75 Kayleigh Roberts, "The Psychology of Victim-Blaming," *Atlantic*, October 5, 2016, https://www.theatlantic.com/science/archive/2016/10/the-psychology -of-victim-blaming/502661/.

81 Anonymous, "I Went to the Hospital."

85 Christa Desir, interview with the author, May 30, 2018.

89 Norm Stamper, quoted in Andrea Ritchie, "How Some Cops Use the Badge to Commit Sex Crimes," *Washington Post*, January 12, 2018, https://www .washingtonpost.com/outlook/how-some-cops-use-the-badge-to-commit -sex-crimes/2018/01/11/5606fb26-eff3-11e7-b390-a36dc3fa2842_story .html?utm_term=.cbcd1dcf2692.

89 Kimberlé Crenshaw and Andrea Ritchie, "Say Her Name: Resisting Police Brutality against Black Women," African American Policy Forum, July 2015, http://www.aapf.org/sayhernamereport/.

90 "Crime in the United States 2010: Methodology," Federal Bureau of Investigation, accessed October 20, 2017, https://ucr.fbi.gov/crime-in -the-u.s/2010/crime-in-the-u.s.-2010/methodology.

90 Police officer, quoted in Chemaly, "Police Fail Rape Victims."

90 Police officer, quoted in Chemaly.

90 Police officer, quoted in Chemaly.

91 Elizabeth Tsung, "It's Time to Reverse Rape Culture," Rebelle Society, January 30, 2016, http://www.rebellesociety.com/2016/01/30/elizabethtsung -rape-culture/.

91 Corey Rayburn Yung, quoted in Chemaly, "Police Fail Rape Victims."

93 Harding, *Asking for It*, 142.

93–94 Josh Hafner, "The Judge in the Larry Nassar Trial: Incredible Quotes to the Victims and Their Abuser," *USA Today Network*, January 24, 2018, https:// www.usatoday.com/story/news/nation-now/2018/01/24/judge-larry-nassar -trial-incredible-quotes-victims-and-their-abuser/1061691001/.

94 Susan Svriuga and Nick Anderson, "DeVos Decries 'Failed System' on Campus Sexual Assault, Vows to Replace It," *Washington Post*, September 7, 2017, https://www.washingtonpost.com/news/grade-point/wp/2017/09/07 /protesters-gather-anticipating-devos-speech-on-campus-sexual-assault /?utm_term=.c58a017ab955.

95 "Jackson Katz: Violence against Women—It's a Men's Issue," TED Talks video, 17:37, posted May 2013, https://www.ted.com/talks/jackson_katz _violence_against_women_it_s_a_men_s_issue.

95 Stephen Spector, "Vice President Biden Marks Sexual Assault Awareness Month, Announcing It's On Us Progress," *The White House* (blog), April 23, 2015, https://obamawhitehouse.archives.gov/blog/2015/04/23/vice -president-biden-marks-sexual-assault-awareness-month-announcing-it -s-us-progres.

99 Sian Norris, Twitter post, September 9, 2017, 10:41 a.m., https://twitter .com/sianushka/status/906573236338610176.

99 Ijeoma Oluo, Facebook post, September 9, 2017, https://www.facebook .com/ijeoma.oluo/posts/10154681626662676.

99 Toby Meyjes, "Piano Man Ends Bid to Win Back Girlfriend after 'Being Punched in the Head,'" *Metro* (London), September 12, 2017, http://metro .co.uk/2017/09/12/piano-man-ends-bid-to-win-back-girlfriend-after-being -punched-in-the-head-6920857/.

100 Anna North, "The Aziz Ansari Story Is Ordinary. That's Why We Have to Talk about It," Vox, January 16, 2018, https://www.vox.com/identities /2018/1/16/16894722/aziz-ansari-grace-babe-me-too.

101 Susan Walsh, "Pop Culture Feeds Rape Culture," Hooking Up Smart, January 8, 2016, https://www.hookingupsmart.com/2016/01/08/politics -and-feminism/pop-culture-makes-rape-culture/.

101 Walsh.

101 Maureen Ryan, "The Progress and Pitfalls of Television's Treatment of Rape," *Variety*, December 6, 2016, http://variety.com/2016/tv/features/rape -tv-television-sweet-vicious-jessica-jones-game-of-thrones-1201934910/.

101 Julie Beck, "When Pop Culture Sells Dangerous Myths about Romance," *Atlantic*, January 17, 2018, https://www.theatlantic.com/entertainment /archive/2018/01/when-pop-culture-sells-dangerous-myths-about-romance /549749/.

104 Maggie Jones, "What Teenagers Are Learning from Online Porn," *New York Times*, February 7, 2018, https://www.nytimes.com/2018/02/07 /magazine/teenagers-learning-online-porn-literacy-sex-education.html.

104 Jones.

104 Jones.

104 Jones.

105 Jones.

105 Doug Henry, quoted in Filipovic, "Offensive Feminism," 13.

106 California State Senate, "Student Safety: Sexual Assault of 2014," Senate Bill 967, September 28, 2014, https://leginfo.legislature.ca.gov/faces /billTextClient.xhtml?bill_id=201320140SB967.

106 Harding, *Asking for It*, 217–218.

106–107 Rebecca Traister, "Why Sex That's Consensual Can Still Be Bad. And Why We're Not Talking about It," *Cut*, October 20, 2015, https://www.thecut .com/2015/10/why-consensual-sex-can-still-be-bad.html.

107 Al Vernacchio, *For Goodness Sex: Changing the Way We Talk to Teens about Sexuality, Values, and Health* (New York: HarperCollins, 2014), 52.

109 Audience member, quoted in Harding, *Asking for It*, 41.

109 Roxane Gay, "Daniel Tosh and Rape Jokes: Still Not Funny," Salon, July 12, 2012, https://www.salon.com/2012/07/12/daniel_tosh_and_rape_jokes _still_not_funny/.

109 Lindy West, "How to Make a Rape Joke," *Jezebel*, July 12, 2012, https:// jezebel.com/5925186/how-to-make-a-rape-joke.

109–110 John Mulaney, quoted in West.

111 Chris Linder and Jessica Harris, "Power-Conscious Approaches to Campus Sexual Violence," Inside Higher Ed, December 1, 2017, https://www .insidehighered.com/advice/2017/12/01/understanding-role-power-plays -campus-sexual-assaults-essay.

111–112 Swati Avasthi, Facebook post, February 27, 2018, https://www.facebook .com/swatiavasthi/posts/10215376575423173.

112 Rebecca Eisenberg, "Finally! An Anti-Rape Campaign That Isn't Victim Blame-y," Upworthy, July 11, 2012, http://www.upworthy.com/finally-an -anti-rape-campaign-that-isnt-victim-blame-y.

112 Daniel Victor, "Janelle Monáe Brings a 'Time's Up' Message to the Grammy Awards," *New York Times*, January 28, 2018, https://www .nytimes.com/2018/01/28/arts/music/janelle-monae-kesha-grammy-awards -metoo.html.

113 Alissa Ackerman and Jill Levenson, "Sexual Assault: A Restorative Justice Model," *Alissa R. Ackerman* (blog), accessed June 26, 2018, http://www .alissaackerman.com/blog/2018/1/28/sexual-assault-a-restorative-justice -model.

113 Claire Chung, quoted in Ackerman and Levenson.

114 "Jackson Katz," TED Talks, video.

115 "Jackson Katz."

116 Emma Brockes, "Me Too Founder Tarana Burke: 'You Have to Use Your Privilege to Serve Other People,'" *Guardian* (US edition), January 15, 2018, https://www.theguardian.com/world/2018/jan/15/me-too-founder-tarana -burke-women-sexual-assault.

118–119 Kate Willett, Twitter post, December 10, 2017, 1:32 p.m., https://twitter .com/katewillett/status/939971100674609152.

119 Terry Crews, "How Terry Crews Escaped the 'Cult of Masculinity,'" Oprah.com, February 13, 2018, http://www.oprah.com/inspiration/how -terry-crews-escaped-the-cult-of-masculinity.

120 Holly Westlund, online interview with the author, Facebook, March 12, 2018.

120 Jim Burkhart, online interview with the author, Facebook, March 12, 2018.

120 Kristi Wallace Knight, online interview with the author, Facebook, March 12, 2018.

120 Mira Reisberg, online interview with the author, Facebook, March 12, 2018.

120 Wendy Myers, online interview with the author, Facebook, March 12, 2018.

120 Cindy Collins Taylor, online interview with the author, Facebook, March 12, 2018.

121 Anne Estes Hearn, online interview with the author, Facebook, March 12, 2018.

121 Kiersi Burkhart, online interview with the author, Facebook, March 12, 2018.

121 T. Edward Bak, online interview with the author, Facebook, March 12, 2018.

121 Andrew Stoehr, online interview with the author, Facebook, March 12, 2018.

121 DeAnna Smith, online interview with the author, Facebook, March 12, 2018.

121 Janice Garceau, online interview with the author, Facebook, March 12, 2018.

Glossary

ableism: discrimination against disabled people, taking the form of treating disabled people as defective or less than human

abstinence: the choice to not engage in sexual behaviors, usually before marriage, though sometimes as a lifelong choice

adultification: expecting nonage-appropriate, adultlike behavior, especially sexual behavior, from certain groups of young people, usually nonwhite children; attributing such behavior to them

adultism: discrimination by adults against teens, mostly through dismissing the opinions of teens and treating them as less important than adults

ally: a person who uses privilege to support others from marginalized groups who face oppression and discrimination

cisgender: a person whose gender identity and biological sex match

cis-sexism: a form of transphobia that regards cisgender people as normal and transgender people as unnatural

classism: discrimination against people based on the social class to which they belong

consent: the active and affirmative decision to participate in sexual acts with another person

feminism: the belief that all genders should have equal access to political, economic, and social power

gender nonconforming: having a gender identity that does not fit into the category of man or woman and may not match one's biological sex

heterosexism: the assumption that heterosexuality is normal and homosexuality is defective

homophobia: hatred or fear of lesbian, gay, bisexual, transgender, queer or questioning, and other (LGBTQ+) peoples

hypersexualization: stereotyping certain groups of people, often black women or gay men, as oversexed or promiscuous

intersectional feminism: an approach to achieving gender equality that recognizes the complex dynamics of overlapping forms of discrimination (such as racism, sexism, ableism, adultism, classism, and homophobia)

intersectionality: the way in which various forms of discrimination (such as racism, sexism, ableism, adultism, classism, and homophobia) overlap and interact

male sexual entitlement: men believing that they have a guaranteed right to sexual attention from and sexual access to women

misogyny: hatred of women, often taking the form of crude jokes and the dismissal of women's abilities and skills

objectification: viewing a body as a sexualized thing rather than as a person. In rape cultures, women are objectified, often through advertising and pop culture.

privilege: opportunities and advantages available to some people but not others based exclusively on qualities such as race, class, or gender that are not earned

racism: discrimination against people of color. It generally takes the form of inequality of pay, unequal access to good schools, segregation of neighborhoods, and unequal treatment by law enforcement.

rape: unwanted penetration of the vagina, mouth, or anus by a penis, a finger, or another type of object

rape culture: a set of widespread beliefs and practices that normalizes and excuses male sexual aggression and violence. Rape culture is supported by laws, pop culture, social expectations, and rigid gender norms.

sexism: discrimination against women based on gender. It takes many forms, from inequalities in pay and restricted access to health care to hurtful language and assault.

sexual aggression: verbal and physical behaviors of a sexual nature that persist even when people being approached say they are not interested

sexual assault: any unwelcome sexual contact or behavior, including rape

sexual harassment: unwelcome sexual comments, images, and behaviors, especially by a person in authority toward a subordinate

slut shaming: using slurs about promiscuity to demean women for the way they dress or behave

statutory rape: sexual acts that occur between an adult and a minor (person below the age of consent); also in some states, sex between two minors

toxic masculinity: a definition of manhood characterized by aggression, dominance, sexual conquest, and a lack of emotional openness

transgender: having a gender identity that does not match a person's biological sex

victim blaming: speech or actions that imply that responsibility for a crime is with the survivor rather than the perpetrator

Selected Bibliography

Beck, Julie. "When Pop Culture Sells Dangerous Myths about Romance." *Atlantic*, January 17, 2018. https://www.theatlantic.com/entertainment/archive/2018/01 /when-pop-culture-sells-dangerous-myths-about-romance/549749/.

Burnett, Zaron. "A Gentleman's Guide to Rape Culture." Huffington Post, June 5, 2014. https://www.huffingtonpost.com/zaron-burnett/guide-to-rape-culture _b_5440553.html

Chemaly, Soraya. "How Police Still Fail Rape Victims." *Rolling Stone*, August 16, 2016. https://www.rollingstone.com/culture/features/how-police-still-fail-rape -victims-w434669.

Farrow, Ronan. "Overtures to Sexual Assault: Harvey Weinstein's Accusers Tell Their Stories." *New Yorker*, October 10, 2017. https://www.newyorker.com/news/news -desk/from-aggressive-overtures-to-sexual-assault-harvey-weinsteins-accusers-tell -their-stories.

Friedman, Jaclyn, and Jessica Valenti, eds. *Yes Means Yes: Visions of Female Sexual Power and a World without Rape.* Berkeley, CA: Seal, 2008.

Harding, Kate. *Asking for It: The Rise of Rape Culture—and What We Can Do about It.* Boston: Da Capo Lifelong Books, 2015.

Kantor, Jodi, and Megan Twohey. "Harvey Weinstein Paid Off Sexual Harassment Accusers for Decades." *New York Times*, October 5, 2017. https://www.nytimes .com/2017/10/05/us/harvey-weinstein-harassment-allegations.html.

Simpson, Connor. "The Steubenville Victim Tells Her Story." *Atlantic*, March 16, 2013. https://www.theatlantic.com/national/archive/2013/03/steubenville-victim -testimony/317302/.

Smith, Joanne, Mandy Van Deven, and Meghan Huppuch. *Hey, Shorty! A Guide to Combating Sexual Harassment and Violence in Schools and on the Streets.* New York: Feminist, 2011.

Smith, S. G., J. Chen, K. C. Basile, L. K. Gilbert, M. T. Merrick, N. Patel, M. Walling, and A. Jain. *The National Intimate Partner and Sexual Violence Survey (NIPSVS): 2010–2012 State Report.* Atlanta: National Center for Injury Prevention and Control, Centers for Disease Control and Prevention, 2017.

Stamp, Nicole. "What Decent Men Can Do in Response to #MeToo." *CNN*, October 23, 2017. http://www.cnn.com/2017/10/21/opinions/what-men-can-do-me-too -stamp-opinion/index.html.

Further Information

Nonfiction Books

Cappiello, Katie, and Meg McInerney, eds. *Slut: A Play and Guidebook for Combating Sexism and Sexual Violence*. New York: Feminist, 2015.

Cronn-Mills, Kirstin. *Transgender Lives: Complex Stories, Complex Voices*. Minneapolis: Twenty-First Century Books, 2015.

Gay, Roxane. *Bad Feminist*. New York: Grove, 2017.

Gay, Roxane, ed. *Not That Bad: Dispatches from Rape Culture*. New York: Harper Perennial, 2018.

Higgins, Nadia Abushanab. *Feminism: Reinventing the F-Word*. Minneapolis: Twenty-First Century Books, 2016.

Jensen, Kelly. *Here We Are: Feminism for the Real World*. Chapel Hill, NC: Algonquin Young Readers, 2017.

Keyser, Amber, ed. *The V-Word: True Stories of First-Time Sex*. New York: Simon Pulse, 2015.

Krakauer, Jon. *Missoula: Rape and the Justice System in a College Town*. New York: Doubleday, 2015.

McGowan, Rose. *Brave*. New York: HarperOne, 2018.

Prout, Chessy. *I Have the Right To: A High School Survivor's Story of Sexual Assault, Justice, and Hope*. New York: Margaret K. McElderry Books, 2018.

Solnit, Rebecca. *Men Explain Things to Me*. Chicago: Haymarket Books, 2015.

Stoian, Marian. *Take It as a Compliment*. Philadelphia: Singing Dragon, 2015.

Waldal, Elin Stebbins. *Tornado Warning: A Memoir of Teen Dating Violence and Its Effect on a Woman's Life*. Encinitas, CA: Sound Beach, 2011.

West, Lindy. *Shrill*. New York: Hachette Books, 2016.

Wittenstein, Vicki Oransky. *Reproductive Rights: Who Decides?* Minneapolis: Twenty-First Century Books, 2016.

Novels about Rape Culture

Anderson, Laurie Halse. *Speak*. New York: Farrar, Straus & Giroux, 1999. One of the first young adult novels to show the devastating effects of a brutal assault.

Arnold, Elana. *Damsel*. New York: Balzer + Bray, 2018. Set in a fairy-tale world, this book takes a searing look at sexual predation, rape culture, and misogyny.

Blount, Patty. *Some Boys*. Naperville, IL: Sourcebooks Fire, 2014. After an assault, a town turns against the survivor.

Burkhart, Kiersi. *Honor Code*. Minneapolis: Carolrhoda Lab, 2018. A girl pursues justice at an elite school that would rather ignore rampant sexual abuse.

Johnston, E. K. *Exit, Pursued by a Bear*. New York: Dutton Books for Young Readers, 2016. A survivor refuses to be defined by her rape.

Mathieu, Jennifer. *Moxie*. New York: Roaring Brook, 2017. A girl takes on the culture of toxic masculinity at her school.

McGinnis, Mindy. *The Female of the Species*. New York: Katherine Tegen Books, 2016. Society might let boys and men get away with sex crimes, but this girl won't.

Reed, Amy. *The Nowhere Girls*. New York: Simon Pulse, 2017. Three misfits take on misogyny at their school.

Summers, Courtney. *All the Rage*. New York: St. Martin's Griffin, 2015. In a culture that refuses to protect its young girls from sexual assault, how can they survive?

Websites

Black Girls Rock
> http://blackgirlsrock.com/
> Black Girls Rock offers mentorship, leadership camps, conferences, events, music, and media to empower and inspire black teens.

Center for Changing Our Campus Culture
> http://changingourcampus.org/
> The Center for Changing Our Campus Culture conducts research and offers solutions intended to end gender-based violence on college campuses.

End the Backlog
> http://www.endthebacklog.org/
> This organization works to raise awareness of and eliminate the rape kit backlog in the United States.

End Rape on Campus
> http://endrapeoncampus.org/
> End Rape on Campus provides direct support for survivors and their communities, offers educational programs designed to reduce sexual assault, and lobbies for policy reform at the campus, local, state, and federal levels.

Everyday Sexism Project
> https://everydaysexism.com/
> The Everyday Sexism Project catalogs instances of sexism experienced on a day-to-day basis. You can follow the project on Twitter too: @EverydaySexism.

Innocence Project

https://www.innocenceproject.org/

The Innocence Project uses genetic evidence to exonerate (undo a wrongful conviction) and gain release from prison for the innocent. The organization also educates the public about wrongful incarceration.

Mentors in Violence Prevention

https://www.mvpstrat.com/

Mentors in Violence Prevention offers educational and workplace programs designed to end sexual harassment, bullying, and gender-based violence.

Microaggressions

http://www.microaggressions.com/

Microaggressions documents daily demonstrations of power, privilege, discrimination, and oppression in everyday life.

Project Unbreakable

http://projectunbreakable.tumblr.com/

Project Unbreakable is a photography project aiming to give a voice to survivors of sexual assault, domestic violence, and child abuse.

Rape Kit Action Project

http://www.everykitcounts.org/

This group advocates for state-by-state legal reforms such as requiring states to track the number of untested rape kits, establishing clear policies on rape kit testing requirements, and creating a plan to test all untested kits.

Sentencing Project

https://www.sentencingproject.org/

The Sentencing Project works to reform racially unjust policies and practices in the US legal system and raise awareness about mass incarceration.

Stop Street Harassment

http://www.stopstreetharassment.org

Stop Street Harassment is a nonprofit organization dedicated to documenting and ending gender-based street harassment worldwide.

UnSlut Project

http://www.unslutproject.com/

Emily Lindin, who was brutally slut shamed in elementary school, founded this project to undo slut shaming and sexual bullying in schools, communities, media, and culture.

Films

The Hunting Ground. DVD. Los Angeles: Chain Camera Pictures, 2015.
This award-winning exposé of rape crimes on US college campuses investigates the way institutions cover up the problem and the harm this does to students and their families.

The Invisible War. DVD. Los Angeles: Chain Camera Pictures, 2012.
This investigative documentary explores the epidemic of the rape of female soldiers within the US military.

The Mask You Live In. DVD. Ross, CA: Representation Project, 2015.
This documentary explores how the narrow definition of masculinity in American culture harms boys, men, and society at large. The film also discusses ideas for making positive change.

Miss Representation. DVD. San Francisco: Girls' Club Entertainment, 2011.
This documentary documents the underrepresentation of women in positions of power and influence in the United States. It challenges the media's limited portrayal of what it means to be a powerful woman.

Tough Guise. DVD. Northampton, MA: Media Education Foundation, 1999.
This documentary examines the relationship between pop-culture imagery and masculine identities in the United States in the twenty-first century.

UnSlut: A Documentary Film. Short film. Los Angeles: The UnSlut Project, 2015.
This award-winning documentary short reveals the causes and devastating effects of slut shaming, sexual bullying, and gender-based discrimination.

Videos

"Al Vernacchio: Sex Needs a New Metaphor. Here's One . . ." TED Talks video, 8:18. Posted July 15, 2013. https://www.ted.com/talks/al_vernacchio_sex_needs_a _new_metaphor_here_s_one/discussion
In this video, Al Vernacchio suggests a new metaphor for sex, one that's about shared pleasure, discussion and agreement, fulfillment and enjoyment.

"Day One 'Sunshine.'" Vimeo video, 2:46. Posted by Guiherme Marcondes, February 13, 2018. https://vimeo.com/255418635.
This short film explores dating and intimate-partner violence.

"Jackson Katz: Violence against Women—It's a Men's Issue." TED Talks video, 17:37. Posted May 29, 2013. https://www.ted.com/talks/jackson_katz_violence_against _women_it_s_a_men_s_issue
Domestic violence and sexual abuse are often called "women's issues." Jackson Katz points out that they are actually men's issues and shows how these violent behaviors are tied to toxic definitions of manhood.

"Oregon School Dress Codes." YouTube video, 8:59. Posted by National Education Association, January 5, 2016. https://www.youtube.com/watch?v=r7G7KXDI4vI. This video documents the testimony of middle-school students in Oregon against discriminatory dress codes. Their work was instrumental in eliminating double standards from the dress code in Oregon's largest school district.

"The Sexy Lie: Caroline Heldman at TEDxYouth@SanDiego." YouTube video, 12:49. Posted by TEDxYouth, January 20, 2013. https://www.youtube.com/watch?time _continue=2&v=kMS4VJKekW8
In this video, national figure Caroline Heldman discusses how the mainstream media contributes to the underrepresentation of women in positions of power and influence in the United States.

"Shelved. 60 Seconds." YouTube video, 1:00. Posted by "Joyful Heart Foundation," February 13, 2018. https://youtu.be/Eu0IwAUwsZQ.
This public service announcement raises awareness of the rape kit backlog.

Hashtags

#everydaysexism
Women describe their day-to-day experiences with sexism and misogyny.

#MeToo
People of all genders share their stories of sexual harassment and assault.

#rapeculture
These posts detail elements of rape culture in daily life.

#SayHerName
Tweets at this hashtag are in remembrance of black women killed by police.

#WhatIWasWearing
Rape survivors describe the clothes they were wearing at the time of the assault.

#YesAllWomen
Women document times when men behaved as if they were entitled to attention and sexual favors.

Index

ableism, 14, 24, 63, 111

Black Lives Matter, 88–89
bullying, 5, 10–11, 36, 47, 56
    bystander action, 43 64, 77, 117
    See also slut shaming
Combined DNA Index System (CODIS), 82,
    83–84
consent, 10, 15, 34, 71, 75, 83, 104, 109
    affirmative, 106, 112, 114
    age-of-consent laws, 105
    and alcohol, 66, 71, 106
    close-in-age exemptions, 105
    definition of, 7, 106
    Yes Means Yes laws, 106

dress codes, 32
    and double standards, 49–51, 54–55, 114
    gender-neutral, 51
    messages behind, 49
    and sexual harassment, 49
    violations of, 49, 51

Fazlalizadeh, Tatyana
    and *She's Gotta Have It*, 38
    and *Stop Telling Women to Smile* protest
        art, 38
femininity, 14, 36, 116
    definition of, 32
    and gender norms, 32–33, 35, 47
feminism, 21, 37, 57, 67, 107, 110
    definition of, 22–23
    and male allies, 24, 114
    and Wild Feminists, 24
    Word of the Year (2017), 23
feminist movement
    and Declaration of Sentiments, 21
    and Frederick Douglass, 21
    Seneca Falls Convention, 21
feminist theorists and theory
    Susan Brownmiller, 19
    The Feminine Mystique (Friedan), 11
    Betty Friedan, 11–12
    Kate Harding, 67, 72, 93, 106
    Mary Ann McClintock, 21

    Lucretia Mott, 21
    Elizabeth Cady Stanton, 21
    Martha Wright, 21
flirting, 43, 49, 67–68, 70, 78, 96, 117–118

gender, 9, 14, 22, 23, 27, 31, 55, 73
    binary model of, 14, 32, 35, 47, 107
    and biology, 22, 31–33
    gender identity, 22, 30–31, 33, 35–36,
        51, 89
    gender norms, 13, 31–33, 35–36, 37, 47,
        56, 102–103, 113, 119
    and neuroscience, 32
Girls for Gender Equity, 11, 41–42
    Joanne Smith, 73
Golden Globe Awards (2018), 14, 26–27

homophobia, 14, 24, 36, 51, 63, 73, 89, 102,
    111

infographics, 54, 103
interracial marriage
    and *Loving v. Virginia*, 79
intersectionality, 36, 55, 77
    definition of, 22
    and feminism, 22
    and rape culture, 23

Joyful Heart Foundation
    and End the Backlog, 86
    and Mariska Hargitay, 86

masculinity, 14–15, 47, 99
    definition of, 32
    and gender norms, 32–33
    and Good Men Project, 35
    toxic, 15, 35–37, 52, 113, 116
men of color, 21, 26, 89
    Cory Batey sentence, 77–79
    and sexual myths, 67, 79, 93
    and wrongful convictions, 78
#MeToo movement, 17–19, 25, 27, 53, 110,
    117
    Tarana Burke, 14, 26, 116
    Alyssa Milano, 17
misogyny, 22–23, 36, 50, 53, 55, 73, 77, 104,

107, 111, 117
definition of, 14
and rape culture, 53, 115–116

Nassar, Larry, 64–66
  and Rosemarie Aquilina, 93
  charges against, 65
  Michigan State University victim
    settlement, 65
  trial of, 65
  verdict and sentence, 65
  victim impact statements, 65–66
National Sexual Assault Hotline, 83

objectification, 49, 57, 59, 101–102, 114
  in ads, 45
  definition of, 45
  and dehumanization, 47
  impact of, 35, 47
  internalized, 47
  and mental health, 47
  in pop culture, 35, 45–46, 57

patriarchy, 21, 23, 36, 46, 55, 57, 72,
    111–112, 114
  definition of, 14, 19
  and rape culture, 71
police, 5–6, 7, 68, 81–85, 94, 117
  believing rape victims, 61–64, 87
  and bias, 24, 87, 92
  handling rape cases, 62
  and people of color, 61, 88–89, 113
  and racism, 24, 88–89
  reforming police response to sexual assault
    cases, 91–93, 112
  sexual assault training, 87, 91–92
  as sexual predators, 72, 89–90
  and shootings, 88
  unfounding rape cases, 90
pop culture, 8, 15, 19, 27, 45–48, 56–57,
    99–100, 106, 114
  Geena Davis Institute on Gender in Media,
    47
  The Handmaid's Tale, 23
  Jane the Virgin, 50
  and music videos, 45–46

Pulp Fiction, 8
She's Gotta Have It (Netflix TV series), 38
Thirteen Reasons Why, 10–11
Twilight (Meyer), 100
Wonder Woman, 23
protest art, 46
  Stop Telling Women to Smile, 38
  "What Were You Wearing?," 74

rape
  accurate language about, 14, 95–96
  arrest and conviction rates, 61, 78, 93
  cultural attitudes toward, 9–10, 12
  definition of, 9, 68
  demographics, 9, 23
  false reports, 61–63, 87
  impact of, 65, 72
  jokes about, 13, 54, 100, 109–110, 116
  and law enforcement, 61–63, 87–92
  and the legal system, 92–94
  and LGBTQ+ peoples, 9, 14, 23, 63, 93
  myths about, 63–64, 72–73, 79, 81,
    93–94, 97
  perpetrator profiles, 19, 73
  as plot point, 101
  and police victim interviews, 61–62, 91
  and power, 17, 19, 22–23, 25–26, 35, 43,
    46, 59, 64, 107, 111, 114, 117
  prevention resources, 42, 83, 95, 114
  and racism, 24, 26, 45, 67, 77–79, 111
  and the Red Zone, 69
  reporting data, 41, 61, 82–83, 90–91, 112
  statistics, 8–9, 13, 23, 61, 63, 73, 78, 87,
    90, 101–102, 109
  Steubenville, OH, case, 5–9
  trauma of, 11, 25, 65–66, 83, 85, 91, 96
  victim advocates, 83, 85, 91–92
  victim blaming, 7–9, 52, 62, 67, 70–71,
    73–75, 90, 95–96, 114
rape cases and perpetrators
  Cory Batey, 77–79
  defense attorney strategy, 8, 70–72, 93
  legal loopholes, 94
  Trent Mays, 5–8
  Larry Nassar, 64–66, 93–94

percentage that go to court, 93
prosecutor strategy, 84, 92–93
Ma'lik Richmond, 5–8
Brock Turner, 68–72, 75–77, 79, 93
rape culture, 49, 52, 63, 69, 71, 81, 90–91, 100
definition of, 12–13, 101
dismantling, steps to, 43, 87, 96, 107, 110, 113–114, 116–117, 119
and language, use of, 14, 95, 102
rape kit, 112
definition of, 82
DNA analysis, 83–85, 87
rape kit backlog
and bias, 87
definition of, 85
Joyful Heart Foundation, 86
Rape Kit Action Project, 86
reasons for, 87, 90
rapists, 8–9, 19, 63–64, 71–73, 95–97
profile of, 84, 87
as serial predators, 61, 84

#SayHerName, 89
sexual assault
on campuses, 42, 68–69, 71, 94–95
definition of, 10
elimination of, 23, 107, 111–117
forensic exam, 81–84
Mentors in Violence Prevention, 34, 114–115
National Sexual Assault Hotline, 83
online postings, 5–7
Violence Against Women Act, 81–82
sexual education programs
abstinence-only, 50, 102–103, 106
accuracy of information, 102–103
curricula, 50–51, 102
history of, 102
and homophobia, 102
infographic, 103
success of, 102–103
Al Vernacchio, 104, 107
sexual empowerment, 57
definition of, 59
sexual entitlement

definition of, 53
examples of, 53, 99
Isla Vista killer, 53
Luke Howard, 99
violence related to, 53–54
sexual harassment
definition of, 10
examples of, 5–7, 10–11, 17–20, 24–26, 33–34, 37–39, 52, 99–101
and male victims, 9, 13, 25
online, 5–7, 13, 54, 109
prevention policies, 41, 112
strategies to combat, 42–43, 111–119
and Title IX, 41
slut shaming, 102, 114
and boys, 55
comebacks, 56
definition of, 55
and girls, 10–11, 39, 55–56, 66–68, 101
solutions
dismantling rape culture, 14–15, 96, 107, 110, 113–114, 117, 119
language reforms, 95–97, 113
police reforms, 91–92, 112
teen activism, 42–43, 50–51
training, 87, 91, 112

teens and sex
impact of sexual harassment, 11
and online pornography, 103–106
and sexual education, 50–51, 102–106
and sexual harassment, 11, 34–36, 40–43, 49, 73
Time, The Silence Breakers (2017), 20
Time's Up, 26, 110
and Oprah Winfrey, 27
Title IX
protections of, 40–41, 94
rescinding protections of, 94
transphobia, 14, 23–24, 47, 73, 89, 93, 111
Trump, Donald
and *Access Hollywood* audiotape, 24, 33
and male sexual entitlement, 33–35
Trump Tag, 33–35, 37

Turner, Brock
  and Cory Batey sentence, 77–79
  and campus drinking culture, 71–72
  defense case, 70–72
  Emily Doe's victim impact statement,
    68–69, 72
  rape trial of, 68
  recall of judge, 76
  verdict and sentence, 68, 75–76

victim blaming, 7–9, 52, 62, 67, 71, 73–75,
  90, 95–96, 114

Weinstein, Harvey, 110–111
  and #MeToo movement, 17–20, 25–27
  New Yorker coverage, 17
  New York Times coverage, 17
women of color, 14, 24, 61, 88–89
  and adultification, 67
  and hypersexualization, 67–68
  and objectification, 45
  and rape, 19, 45, 67
Women's March on Washington (2017), 23
wrongful convictions, 78

#YesAllWomen, 52–54

Photo Acknowledgments

Image credits: Hero Images/Getty Images, p. 6; REUTERS/Keith Srakocic/
Pool/Newscom, p. 7; Bettmann/Getty Images, pp. 12, 78; Chelsea Guglielmino/
FilmMagic/Getty Images, p. 20; Mike Coppola/Getty Images for Busboys and Poet,
p. 22; Emma McIntyre/Getty Images for Los Angeles Dodgers Foundation/agency,
p. 25; Paul Drinkwater/NBCUniversa/Getty Images, p. 27; Jan Stromme/Stone/
Getty Images, p. 30; Inspiring/Shutterstock.com, p. 31; Ben Gabbe/Getty Images for
Paramount Network/Getty Images, p. 38; Vicky Kasala/DigitalVision/Getty Images,
p. 40; Jenny Matthews/Alamy Stock Photo, p. 42; M.Sobreira/Alamy Stock Photo,
p. 46; Denise Truscello/Getty Images, p. 48; Gregory Rec/Portland Press Herald/
Getty Images, p. 50; Laura Westlund/Independent Picture Service, pp. 54, 103;
Robin Skjoldborg/DigitalVision/Getty Images, p. 58; AF archive/Alamy Stock Photo,
p. 62; GEOFF ROBINS/AFP/Getty Images, p. 65; Bill Clark/CQ Roll Cal/Getty
Images, p. 66; San Jose Mercury News/Tribune News Service/Getty Images, p. 70;
VALERIE MACON/AFP/Getty Images, p. 73; AP Photo/Paul Elias, p. 76; AP Photo/
Samuel M. Simpkins/The Tennessean, p. 77; Ann Hermes/The Christian Science
Monitor/Getty Images, p. 82; Denver Post, Inc./Denver Post/Getty Images, p. 84;
Tony Barson/FilmMagic/Getty Images, p. 86; Keith Getter/Moment Mobile ED/
Getty Images, p. 88; New York Daily News/Getty Images, p. 89; Mirrorpix, p. 100;
FilmMagic/agency/Getty Images, p. 110; David Schaffer/Caiaimage/Getty Images,
p. 115; Sam Edwards/OJO Images/Getty Images, p. 118.

About the Author

Evolutionary biologist-turned-author Amber J. Keyser has an MS in zoology and a PhD in genetics. Her young adult novels include *The Way Back from Broken*, an exploration of grief and the healing power of wilderness, and *Pointe, Claw*, a novel about claiming the territory of the body. Her most recent young adult nonfiction titles are *Underneath It All: A History of Women's Underwear*, *Sneaker Century: A History of Athletic Shoes*, *Tying the Knot: A World History of Marriage*, and *The V-Word*, an anthology of personal essays by women about first-time sex. More information is available at www.amberjkeyser.com and on Twitter at @amberjkeyser.